"Together Köstenberger, Bock, and Chatr[...] skeptic Bart Ehrman of the University of North [...] many extravagant claims about Scripture as te[...], [...], [...] with contradictions, partly forged, and unable to provide meaningful answers to the question of human suffering. In response, these authors take up Ehrman's challenge and show that, on closer reflection, Ehrman is telling a very selective and skewed story. Truth matters, and this trio of authors succeed in showing that the truth of the Christian faith can stand up to the most arduous of critics. A great resource for sobering up people who are drunk on new wine from Chapel Hill."

—*Michael F. Bird, lecturer in Theology,*
Ridley Melbourne Mission and Ministry College, Australia

"Disturbed by the numerous attacks on the historic Christian faith by Bart Ehrman's revisionist writings? This wonderful book offers a one-stop-shopping refutation of virtually all of them. Never heard of Ehrman but concerned about how the Bible originated, how faithfully it was copied, if it is full of contradictions, how to respond to the problem of evil and related questions? Köstenberger, Bock, and Chatraw demolish the main contentions of skepticism in each of the areas they address—essential reading!"

—*Craig L. Blomberg, distinguished professor of New Testament, Denver Seminary*

"I can't stress how needed *Truth in a Culture of Doubt* is. It hits the bulls-eye by targeting the exact questions so many people are asking today. I'm so thankful for trusted, scholarly, but very practical responses to these critical questions. I hope as many people read this book as possible, as so much is at stake. What a wonderful resource for the church."

—*Dan Kimball, pastor, Vintage Faith Church, Santa Cruz, California*

"Over the last number of years, Bart Ehrman has proven to be one of Christianity's most persistent critics. In book after book, he has challenged Christianity's most cherished beliefs about Jesus and the reliability of the New Testament. I am so thankful that we now have this excellent full-length response to his claims. Köstenberger, Bock, and Chatraw dismantle the attacks of Ehrman one by one, showing not only that the New Testament is historically reliable but also that its teachings are coherent and consistent. In our current cultural climate of doubt and skepticism, this volume is a must read for every Christian."

—*Michael J. Kruger, president and professor of New Testament,*
Reformed Theological Seminary, Charlotte, North Carolina

"Jesus said, while praying to the Father, 'Your word is truth' (John 17:17). Many are skeptical about this claim, and one of the most famous skeptics is Bart Ehrman. The authors of this useful and accessible book demonstrate that belief in the Scriptures does not represent the sacrifice of one's intellect. Many will be strengthened in their faith and encouraged in reading this work."

—*Thomas R. Schreiner, James Buchanan Harrison Professor of New Testament*
Interpretation, The Southern Baptist Theological Seminary

"Christian engagement with today's culture requires attention to both truth and tone. Believers must be prepared to answer skeptical questions about Christian belief but to do so with winsomeness and civility. *Truth in a Culture of Doubt* helps Christians do that. These top-notch scholars respond convincingly to the arguments and assumptions of a skeptic. The result is a tool that will encourage believers in their faith and equip them to engage cynic and seeker with respect and persuasiveness."

—*Ed Stetzer, executive director of LifeWay Research*

"It is an odd thing no doubt, but nonetheless true, that some biblical scholars today subscribe to an upside-down form of the Reformation principle. The Reformation principle, you may remember, insisted on justification by faith. Many academics, such as Bart Ehrman, turn this on its head and insist on justification by doubt. By this I mean that they mistakenly identify critical thinking or 'real scholarly work' with the ability to doubt something or dismiss it as historically improbable. Furthermore, an antisupernatural bias (or a pro-purely naturalistic one) is assumed to be the basis of the modern scholarly study of history. To compound the error, this is called 'objectivity' or 'unbiased critical thinking'! What Ehrman fails to tell you is that the assumption or statement 'miracles don't happen because they cannot happen' is itself a faith statement. No one has such exhaustive knowledge of reality that they could confidently make such a truth claim, much less assume that is the truth. In *Truth in a Culture of Doubt* a variety of good and competent scholars take on some of the basic claims of Bart Ehrman's various books, including the more academic ones, at the historical, theological, and philosophical levels. The result is that it appears the scholarship that is most suffering from truth decay is Ehrman's and the works of those like him, not that of more traditional Christian scholars."

—*Ben Witherington III, Amos Professor of New Testament for Doctoral Studies,*
Asbury Theological Seminary

"In every generation, some manage to ride skepticism of the Bible to fame and even riches. This book calmly, carefully, and convincingly dismantles some of the major claims of Bart D. Ehrman. It will be valuable for college and seminary students who are assigned Ehrman's widely used New Testament introduction. For anyone impacted by the gaudy claims Ehrman makes to have discredited the whole Christian movement and its scriptural basis, this book provides helpful counter-arguments and better ways of viewing the evidence. In that sense it even serves as a discipleship guide to deepen informed Christian belief. It confirms that, skeptics old or new notwithstanding, there are good reasons for continuing to affirm that the Bible is the Word of God."

—*Robert W. Yarbrough, professor of New Testament,*
Covenant Theological Seminary

ENGAGING
SKEPTICAL CHALLENGES
to the BIBLE

TRUTH

in a

CULTURE

of DOUBT

**ANDREAS J. KÖSTENBERGER,
DARRELL L. BOCK,
and JOSH D. CHATRAW**

B&H
PUBLISHING GROUP
NASHVILLE, TENNESSEE

978-1-4336-8404-3

Published by B&H Publishing Group
Nashville, Tennessee

Dewey Decimal Classification: 220.1
Subject Heading: BIBLE—CRITICISM \ BIBLE—EVIDENCES,
AUTHORITY, ETC. \ CHRISTIANITY—APOLOGETIC WORKS

Printed in the United States of America

1 2 3 4 5 6 7   •   18 17 16 15 14
VP

From Andreas:
For David as you head toward college.
For Timothy as you head toward high school.
You are the best sons a father could ask for. I love you!
"I have no greater joy than this: to hear that my
children are walking in the truth" (3 John 4).
And for my students and mentees over the past two decades of
full-time teaching, with gratitude for your faithful service.

From Darrell:
To all the Hendricks Center Table podcast team at Dallas
Seminary: Andy, Pam, Kym, Mikel, Katie, Heather, Ryan, and
Jonathan. You all know what these topics mean to people.

From Josh:
For Tracy. I love you.

From all of us:
To the people at LifeWay: Jim Baird, David Schroeder,
Chris Cowan, Jeremy Howard, and Micah Carter.
To ministries like Cru, Young Life, Navigators, Ratio
Christi, Campus Outreach, and Christian Union,
plus other campus organizations—your work on
university campuses impacts generations.

CONTENTS

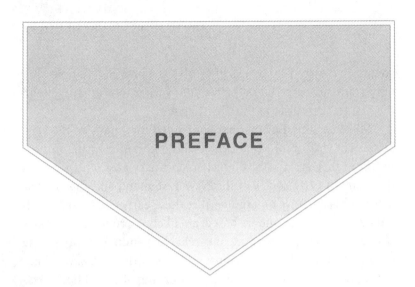

PREFACE

Perhaps you've seen one of Bart Ehrman's debate performances against a variety of opponents. Maybe you've read one of his many best-selling books. You may even have taken a class with Professor Ehrman. Or perhaps you've never even heard of him. No matter what your level of acquaintance with Bart Ehrman and his writings, the issues he raises are important for the faith.

In this book we take a closer look at some of the key arguments Ehrman keeps repeating in radio interviews, in debates, and in his growing number of works. If you're looking for real answers to Ehrman's arguments from a biblical perspective, easily accessible and thoughtfully presented, this book is for you.

Over the years Ehrman has attacked the Bible from what may seem like every conceivable angle. His story is well known. He started out at Moody Bible Institute before attending Wheaton College and later Princeton University, where one of his professors helped him conclude there might be errors in the Bible. What followed was a journey from faith to ever-increasing skepticism and eventual agnosticism.

In his efforts to discredit historic Christianity, Ehrman has methodically sought to dismantle virtually every major plank in the Christian religion. In his earlier writings he strenuously argued that at the root the gospel was not based on the authoritative, commonly agreed-upon teaching of Jesus and his disciples but only gradually emerged as the result of various power struggles in the first few centuries of the Christian era.

More recently Ehrman has contended that many of the New Testament writings were fabricated and not written by the authors to whom they are ascribed. Ehrman's primary area of expertise is the study of early copies of the New Testament, and thus he has focused his energies on arguing that these early copies, on which our current translations are based, are likely corrupt. He expresses strong skepticism regarding the reliable handing down of the original text. He claims that most scholars in the field have all but abandoned the quest for the original wording of the biblical texts.

In addition, Ehrman has also ventured into the area of biblical theology, alleging that there are numerous contradictions in Scripture. In his quest to demonstrate such incongruities, Ehrman has recycled many critical arguments made by liberal biblical scholars in the past, virtually all of which have been answered by conservative scholars. This includes supposed discrepancies among the Gospels, matters of chronology, and other historical or theological differences. Most recently he has claimed that the New Testament itself has contradicting and evolving views on the divinity of Jesus.

Perhaps one of the strongest reasons for Ehrman's aversion to the Christian faith is revealed in his book *God's Problem*, where he states that God's inaction in the face of evil and human suffering is not only unexplainable but inexcusable. How can a good and loving God allow innocent people to suffer? For Ehrman this is inconceivable.

In this book we will take up Ehrman's arguments on these issues one at a time. Not only have we broken Ehrman's skeptical edifice into different units, but we have also isolated specific debating points that recur in Ehrman's public appearances and published writings. After a brief introduction to Ehrman's persona and pilgrimage ("From Fundamentalist to Skeptic"), chapter 1 takes up the question, "Is God Immoral Because He Allows Suffering?" Ehrman claims to have problems with the Bible's trustworthiness, but in his book *God's Problem*, his dissatisfaction with God's way of running the world appears to be Ehrman's biggest problem. In this chapter we show that Christian thinkers have given satisfactory answers to Ehrman's questions, many of which Ehrman hasn't adequately explored in his book.

A fascinating topic is that of biblical theology, that is, the interrelationships between the various books of the Bible. If the chapter on the copying of biblical manuscripts (chapter 3) is played out on Ehrman's home turf, so to speak, in that he is a text critic, chapter 2 is a home game for us in that two of the authors have spent years writing on the subject and have collaborated on a new and growing series, Biblical Theology of the New Testament. Chapter 2, then, squarely faces the question: "Is the Bible Full of Irresolvable Contradictions?" It's here that we'll also address one of the claims of Ehrman's newest book: the New Testament is made up of contradicting Christologies. In essence we conclude that Ehrman is far too quick to rush to judgment and that reasonable explanations are readily available where he cries, "Contradiction!"

Chapter 3, "Are the Biblical Manuscripts Corrupt?" goes to the heart of the matter. Is it true, as Ehrman claims, that the process by which the biblical manuscripts were copied was riddled with errors so that we must lose confidence in the Bible that we have today? Is it true that we no longer have the text of the New Testament and that we have no idea what might have been changed from the originals in the copies that have come down to us? We will show that, again, Ehrman's skeptical outlook has unduly flavored his assessment. We have strong reasons for confidence in the Bible we have.

Chapter 4 continues our response by discussing the question, "Were There Many Christianities?" In this chapter we show that the gospel found in the New Testament was based on the Old Testament expectation of a Messiah fulfilled in Jesus and that this gospel was preached almost immediately after Jesus' death and resurrection.

Chapter 5, "Are Many Biblical Documents Forged?" takes up the matter of the authorship of the New Testament documents. It makes sense for an opponent of Christianity to try to discredit the authors of its foundational writings; but does the evidence, fairly assessed, really bear out Ehrman's skepticism in this regard? In this chapter we show that we have good reason to believe the professed authors are the real authors of the New Testament.

The conclusion deals with "Reasons to Believe." We will see that Ehrman is driven by doubt that raises the bar of proof so high no one will ever satisfy his demands for sufficient evidence for faith. But before we delve into the details of Ehrman's proposals, in our first chapter we'll take a moment to get better acquainted with Ehrman's personal background and spiritual pilgrimage.

Yet you may find yourself asking, "Why discuss Bart Ehrman?" This book is not so much about him but about the positions he represents as the best known, public-square spokesperson for skepticism and the Christian faith. His books have sold everywhere. His texts are used on many campuses around the country. What he writes, people read and repeat. So familiarity with his arguments means one is prepared to engage on a host of questions often raised about the Christian faith. If you want to know what the culture of doubt is, then knowing how to engage with the issues Ehrman raises is imperative.

INTRODUCTION: FROM FUNDAMENTALIST TO SKEPTIC

The Success of Bart Ehrman

As far as biblical scholars go, Bart Ehrman is a rock star. Ehrman is full-time professor at the University of North Carolina at Chapel Hill and adjunct professor at Duke University. He has written numerous scholarly works and holds prestigious posts in academic societies. His scholarly credentials are impressive. Yet none of his professional academic achievements has made Bart Ehrman the near-household name he has become. Ehrman's website lists four books written in the last ten years that have made it on *The New York Times* Best Sellers list.[1] No scholar sells that many books writing academic treatises, even if they could serve as a cure for the millions who suffer from insomnia. Ehrman is anything but boring! He has appeared on television numerous times on such programs as *The Daily Show with John Stewart*, *The Colbert Report*, NBC's *Dateline*, *Inside Edition*, and many others. He travels the world taking part in public debates

---

[1] Bart D. Ehrman, *Misquoting Jesus: The Story Behind Who Changed the Bible and Why* (San Francisco: Harper, 2005); idem, *God's Problem: How the Bible Fails to Answer Our Most Important Question—Why We Suffer* (New York: HarperCollins, 2008); idem, *Jesus, Interrupted: Revealing the Hidden Contradictions in the Bible (And Why We Don't Know About Them)* (San Francisco: HarperOne, 2009); idem, *Forged: Writing in the Name of God—Why the Bible's Authors Are Not Who We Think They Are* (San Francisco, HarperOne, 2011).

and giving lectures. Rarely does a biblical scholar receive this kind of attention from the general public.

So what makes Ehrman so popular? Several factors may explain his rise to fame. Most importantly, he has the ability to explain difficult concepts to a lay audience. In his writing Ehrman is personal, interesting, and at times even surprisingly vulnerable.[2] He has a charismatic personality and writes about the Bible, a book that has been of great interest to believers and nonbelievers for close to 2,000 years. Certainly these factors explain his success in part, but they can't fully account for the flood of attention Ehrman has received. After all, books written by Bible experts for a lay audience are a dime a dozen, but most of them never come close to reaching the sales figures Ehrman's works have achieved or earn the author guest appearances on Comedy Central.

Ehrman is not really an innovator when it comes to theology and the views he presents. He doesn't claim to be. Rather, he summarizes well what other scholars argue concerning the Bible and early Christianity. He is a master at packaging these arguments. He does so in both popular books and texts used in university classes on the New Testament and early Christianity. What you should be aware of is that in presenting these arguments, Ehrman rarely acknowledges counterarguments to his own position. The treatment of a given issue in Ehrman's writings is far more one-sided than the real discussion taking place. This is one thing we hope to show. We suggest two further reasons that have contributed to the Ehrman phenomenon.

First, Ehrman's success is due in large part to the fact that his skeptical biases have led to negative conclusions that are—no surprise—of great interest to other skeptics. Western culture is becoming increasingly hostile to exclusive truth claims. The sentiment is often felt that "everyone can believe anything they want, as long as they aren't saying other people's beliefs are wrong." In his book *The Intolerance of Tolerance*, D. A. Carson has provided numerous

---

[2] In *God's Problem* Ehrman shares there are times he wakes up in the middle of the night in a cold sweat at the prospect that he is wrong and hell is real (p. 127).

examples of how this attitude pervades our society.[3] Carson quotes a recent graduate from Harvard as saying at his commencement:

> They tell us it's heresy to suggest the superiority of some value, fantasy to believe in moral argument, slavery to submit to a judgment sounder than your own. The freedom of our day is freedom to devote yourself to any values we please, on the mere condition that we do not believe them to be true.[4]

Of course, Christianity not only calls for complete devotion, it asks for belief in certain exclusive truths; increasingly, the culture is intolerant toward these claims. The result is mounting cynicism toward Christianity and an eager acceptance of counterclaims that reject historic Christianity (though, ironically, these counterclaims are often also exclusive truth claims).

One of the strengths of Ehrman's writing is his ability to engage an audience by weaving his own journey into many of his books. Ehrman tells of how he was first a fundamentalist and then an evangelical Christian, before adopting his present agnosticism toward God and his skepticism toward the Bible. He attended Moody Bible Institute for three years and then Wheaton College for two—both conservative Christian schools. Ehrman then entered Princeton Seminary, where he eventually earned both a master of divinity and a Ph.D. degree. During his time at Princeton, his views began to change dramatically. Ehrman portrays himself as courageously looking at the evidence and doing what few other conservative Christians are willing to do: face the evidence and give up on the notion of the trustworthiness of the Bible.

Embedded into Ehrman's story, and the story of many other former card-carrying fundamentalists-turned-Bible-critics, is the pervasive skepticism and academic intolerance against faith, particularly Christian faith, they experienced as students at institutions of higher learning.

---

[3] D. A. Carson, *The Intolerance of Tolerance* (Grand Rapids: Eerdmans, 2012).
[4] Ibid., 97.

For instance, Michael V. Fox has insisted that faith-based scholarship of any kind should not be permitted into the forum of biblical scholarship.[5] He allows for people to hold personal religious views but claims their actual scholarship must be "secular." In other words, as long as individuals shed their religious presuppositions and work from secular presuppositions, they can be tolerated.

While this might be shocking to you, Albert Mohler has pointed out, "Fox is simply asserting what many others in the academy have thought for a very long time."[6] George Marsden assesses much of the current academic culture in a similar vein: "One way to describe the current state of affairs, however, is that, in effect, the only points of view that are allowed full academic credence are those that presuppose purely naturalistic worldviews."[7]

The problem with this intolerance, of course, is that all presuppositions are accepted in some sense by faith. Atheists work from the assumption that there is no God. Certainly, this assumption, too, requires a certain amount of faith. To put it another way, some have claimed that the belief in God is inviolable and thus should not be accepted as a premise in scholarship. But is not atheism also inviolable?

In any case Marsden and Mohler are correct in noting the hostility and skepticism at many academic institutions toward religious views. Yet many of these professors and their students who have been critical of religious presuppositions have not been critical enough with their own presuppositions. Is anyone really approaching the Bible without presuppositions that are inviolable?

But according to Ehrman, he simply put aside his biases and faced the facts. In recounting his own personal journey from fundamentalist Christian to agnostic, Ehrman writes, "I kept reverting to my basic question: how does it help us to say that the Bible is the

[5] Michael V. Fox, "Bible Scholarship and Faith-Based Study: My View," accessed October 10, 2013, http://www.sbl-site.org/publications/article.aspx?articleId=490.

[6] Albert Mohler, "Can Believers Be Bible Scholars? A Strange Debate in the Academy," accessed October 10, 2013, http://www.albertmohler.com/2006/03/20/can-believers-be-bible-scholars-a-strange-debate-in-the-academy-2.

[7] George M. Marsden, *The Soul of the American University: From Protestant Establishment to Established Nonbelief* (New York: Oxford University Press, 1996), 430.

inerrant word of God if in fact we don't have the words that God inerrantly inspired, but only the words copied by the scribes— sometimes correctly and sometimes (many times!) incorrectly?"[8] Not only did he begin to lose trust in the biblical manuscript evidence, but this growing skepticism toward the actual content of the Bible proved a pivotal issue in his journey. Ehrman explains that during his work on his master's degree, he came to view the Gospel of Mark as making a mistake in its reference to Abiathar as high priest during a time when Ahimelech was actually the priest (Mark 2:26).[9] Upon concluding that Mark simply made a mistake, he states, "The floodgates opened."[10] For Ehrman the Bible "began to appear to me as a very human book" full of contradictions and errors.[11] However, according to Ehrman, ultimately it wasn't because of what he saw as problems in the Bible that he lost his Christian faith but because, in his own words, "I could no longer explain how there can be a good and all-powerful God actively involved with this world, given the state of things."[12] For this reason Ehrman now says, "I don't 'know' if there is a God; but I think that if there is one, he certainly isn't the one proclaimed by the Judeo-Christian tradition, the one who is actively and powerfully involved in this world."[13]

These quotes from Ehrman not only reveal his own journey in search of truth but also hint at some of Ehrman's own biases and unproven assumptions. We will explore many more of these in the chapters to follow, but consider a few of the assumptions Ehrman makes. For example, he says, "We don't have the words that God inerrantly inspired."[14] He makes this assertion in *Misquoting Jesus* but actually doesn't provide evidence that demonstrates we don't have the original wording in our manuscripts.[15] Or consider his jump after accepting that Mark was possibly in error to the "floodgates opening" to a point where he determined the Bible

---

[8] Ehrman, *Misquoting Jesus*, 7.
[9] Ibid., 9. We deal with this issue in chapter 2 under "Claim 2."
[10] Ibid.
[11] Ibid., 11.
[12] Ehrman, *God's Problem*, 3.
[13] Ibid., 4.
[14] Ehrman, *Misquoting Jesus*, 10.
[15] See chapter 3 for a fuller explanation of this point.

is man's creation rather than divinely inspired. Dan Wallace has commented regarding this part of Ehrman's testimony: "What strikes me as most remarkable in all this is how much Ehrman tied inerrancy to the general historical reliability of the Bible. It was an all-or-nothing proposition for him. He still seems to see things in black-and-white terms. . . . There thus seems to be no middle ground in his view of the text."[16] Wallace wonders if Ehrman's basic approach has changed much from the beginning of his journey until now:

> But from where I sit, it seems that Bart's black-and-white mentality as a fundamentalist has hardly been affected as he slogged through the years and trials of life and learning, even when he came out on the other side of the theological spectrum. He still sees things without sufficient nuancing, he overstates his case, and he is entrenched in the security that his own views are right. Bart Ehrman is one of the most brilliant and creative textual critics I have ever known, and yet his biases are so strong that, at times, he cannot even acknowledge them.[17]

In this book we will try to show that Ehrman's biases lead to his unduly skeptical conclusions. It comes as no surprise that Ehrman has drawn quite a following in the culture in general where so many are looking for reasons to doubt and within an academic culture where the presuppositions of ideological naturalism are held out as the ideal.

The second explanation for Ehrman's appeal to a lay audience is tied to a misunderstanding of what "faith" means in many pockets of Christianity. Faith is understood in different ways in our culture today. One popular conception of faith is that it has nothing (or very little) to do with reason or logic. "After all," some might say, "faith is not something you seek to provide evidence for or view

---

[16] Daniel Wallace, "The Gospel According to Bart: A Review Article of *Misquoting Jesus* by Bart Ehrman," *Journal of the Evangelical Theological Society* 49 (2006): 333.
[17] Ibid., 349.

rationally; you are simply to accept it." This kind of faith sits well in a culture that lauds personal preferences. If faith is not grounded in reason, logic, and historical realities, it is simply a personal preference. Faith is what works for certain kinds of people, and there is no need for evidence. Unfortunately, too often people today have accepted this idea of blind faith. Even while many in the church might not put things so candidly, often Christians, without even realizing it, have embraced an anti-intellectualism that tends to leave the "hard" stuff to the trained scholars.

The Bible, however, does not ask for blind faith. Instead, it calls for a *reasoned* faith, a faith that looks at the evidence. This kind of faith is honest about questions and even personal doubts and looks for real answers. It seeks the best possible explanation and then commits to the truth. Reasoned faith is what Paul describes in 1 Corinthians 15 where he says that Jesus died, was buried, and then was raised from the grave (vv. 3–4). These events either happened or they didn't. If they didn't, Christianity is nothing but a terrible hoax (1 Cor 15:17–19). However, if Jesus was raised from the dead, this calls for a change in the way we think and in the way we live. Paul doesn't ask for blind faith but claims that more than 500 people saw the risen Jesus after his death. It's one thing to say that 500 people saw the risen Jesus, but now those people are dead; it's another to do what Paul does—publicly announce that most of these witnesses are still alive. It would have been easy to prove Paul wrong if these witnesses didn't really exist. Paul has no fear of people following the evidence. In fact, he encourages historical investigation.

All too often Christians, and even pastors, haven't been challenged to think historically and logically. The historical questions about the Bible and the theological questions concerning the God who claims to have inspired the Bible are rarely broached in many churches. Too often Christian scholarship has been kept safely at arm's length and even viewed with suspicion by the church. Speaking and writing into this environment, Bart Ehrman has found a captive audience. In part Ehrman's books seem to have drawn a large following because he's talking about things most people never learned about in church. Some have long given up on Christianity, and Ehrman is only reinforcing their decision to depart from their Christian upbringing. Others are trying to reconcile their faith with reason and find Ehrman's books both interesting and disturbing.

Ehrman knows all too well that the average person in the pew—or in the pub—has little to no knowledge of the historical and theological issues he raises. He has become the tour guide for many on their first-time journey exploring topics such as the Bible's origins, the copying of the Bible, biblical theology, and the relationship between God and evil. As a guide for unsuspecting tourists, Ehrman gets to choose the sites to visit and decide how the stories are told. The sightseers find it all fascinating and are reassured that this is what all the guides—the reasonable ones, anyway—are telling the visitors. For those on a journey investigating these issues for the first time, Ehrman provides his own reasons *not* to trust the Bible. Some of his textbooks even have discussion questions designed to take the reader in this direction. If anyone lacks foundation in dealing with the various biblical or theological topics he raises, Ehrman's guided tours are not only challenging; they can be downright overwhelming. So pastors, theological students, missionaries (Ehrman's books seem to be a pretty big hit in the Middle East as well), and anyone who claims or plans to be a teacher: You can't ignore these issues any longer! You need to ask these questions and help people understand the answers. We have written another book you can give to people that will communicate the ideas you read here to a more popular audience, but we know your people will want to hear these things explained by someone they know and trust.[18] So we have written this book to flesh things out a bit more for those who want to go deeper and be better prepared to equip others.

One of the things we want you to see in this book is that, unfortunately, all too often Ehrman's rhetoric and interpretations conceal more than they reveal. For example, Ehrman's opening chapter in *Jesus, Interrupted* sets out to describe his own journey that led him to distrust the Bible, to provide a list of various

---

[18] *Truth Matters: Confident Faith in a Confusing World* (Nashville: B&H, 2014).

problems in Scripture, and to reassure his readers that he is not alone in reaching such critical conclusions. He writes,

> All of my closest friends (and next-to-closest friends) in the guild of New Testament studies agree with most of my historical views of the New Testament, the historical Jesus, the development of the Christian faith, and other similar issues. We may disagree on this point or that (in fact we do—we are, after all, scholars), but we all agree on the historical methods and the basic conclusions they lead to.[19]

He leaves the impression that his views are standard fare among biblical scholars. Among some circles this is certainly true, but plenty of scholars see things rather differently. Often Ehrman's comments appear to force the readers into accepting his assertions by the mere weight of the unanimity in his circle of scholarship, which he makes out to be the only serious type of scholarship. Ehrman's rhetoric gives him a psychological edge with a lay audience but proves unhelpful in actually dealing with the hard data of the text. This seems a strange way to begin a book for someone claiming to be an unbiased historian.[20]

Whether written for a lay audience or not, a work of scholarship should set out to defend a position against the best of the opposing positions. As will become apparent in subsequent chapters, however, Ehrman has a way of stereotyping scholarship depending on whether it agrees with his own views; he routinely misrepresents, underrepresents, or never represents those who oppose his positions.

So when Ehrman makes statements such as, "I believe that better arguments will win out, if people approach the question without a bias in favor of one view or another," we agree with him in part (though we wonder if Ehrman's ideal of the unbiased

---

[19] Ehrman, *Jesus, Interrupted*, 17.
[20] This observation is noted by Michael J. Kruger, "Review of *Jesus, Interrupted*," accessed April 25, 2012, http://www.reformation21.org/shelf-life/jesus-interrupted.php.

observer is really realistic).[21] Our problem with Ehrman's books is not that *he's* making historical arguments while *we* think people should simply ignore the evidence and believe blindly. Our problem with his books is that we are convinced Ehrman's arguments are not the best ones, and he's done little to acknowledge scholarly alternatives to his positions.

Ehrman has a clever way of dismissing those in the academy whose research has led them to trust in the Bible. On the one hand Ehrman says that logic and evidence are what counts; let the best arguments win. But then he also suggests (sometimes explicitly, sometimes implicitly) that everyone who disagrees with him is biased and that he and those who agree with him are the only ones looking at the evidence objectively.[22] Despite Ehrman's effort to broadly paint all other views as biased, he cannot escape the strokes from his own paintbrush. Does Ehrman really expect his readers to believe he doesn't have biases of his own? Or that he alone has no presuppositions? After his approach has become more evident in the chapters to follow, we will return to these questions in the concluding chapter. In the following pages you'll see that plenty of tour guides offer different and more compelling explanations and that Ehrman isn't exactly the unbiased guide he portrays himself to be.

One should not misunderstand how this discussion works. No one, conservative or liberal, can prove the Bible is true or not with 100-percent certainty. This is a false standard on both sides of the debate. Tracing history that is 2,000 or more years old is too complex to yield such certainty. Rather, what one does in appealing to evidence, reason, and logic is make a case—hopefully the most plausible one—for either believing or doubting Scripture. Ehrman does a solid job of assembling the arguments that can be used to question Scripture and early Christianity, but we think his presentation is one-sided and slides by many important elements in these discussions. These elements impact the deliberations one must make and the judgments all render about the plausibility of

---

[21] Bart D. Ehrman, *Did Jesus Exist? The Historical Argument for Jesus of Nazareth* (San Francisco: HarperOne, 2013), 143.

[22] Ibid., 143–44.

Scripture and whether it gives an accurate portrayal of Jesus and the movement that arose from him.

Ehrman as a Test Case

We haven't written this book to convince Bart Ehrman or other skeptical scholars of our views. Ehrman, we trust, knows most of the information we set forth in these pages and has chosen to follow his own line of reasoning due to a variety of factors. Instead, we are writing for those of you who have encountered Ehrman's arguments (or others like them) and need to better understand the other side of the argument.

In a recent sermon I (Chatraw) talked about some critical views of the Bible held by other university and seminary professors. Afterward, I had a conversation with a dear woman who simply couldn't understand how professors who are experts on the Bible, who spend most of their time teaching and writing about the Bible, don't actually believe it. Later I was a bit surprised when I had a similar discussion with a couple of well-respected pastors in my community. These conversations helped me see once again that most people, even pastors, don't know much about what's going on in the world of biblical scholarship. The other authors of this book have had similar discussions. We often answer that some pursue such study because they love history or ancient history, while others do so to react to their upbringing (much as Ehrman has). Some even do it for both reasons.

These other reasons for studying Christianity are often missed by those whose reason is simply grounded in faith. The reason for this perplexity about the motivations for biblical scholarship is, of course, in part because most are not called to be biblical scholars. However, lack of awareness of foundational historical and theological issues often leaves the nonscholar vulnerable. While this book will focus on responding to Ehrman's objections to the Bible and historic Christianity, Ehrman is not alone in offering the kind of objections you'll see in the following pages. He readily admits that for the most part he has only popularized views that have been around in scholarly discussions for a long time. In this way our response to Ehrman serves as a kind of test case in engaging with skeptical scholarship in general.

While you may never meet Bart Ehrman, you will likely encounter someone who makes similar arguments; or perhaps you yourself have accepted some of Ehrman's arguments as irrefutable. After all, his books haven't made *The New York Times* Best Sellers list for no reason. Ehrman is an accomplished scholar and talented writer who has struck a chord with many. However, in the pages to follow, you will not only see many of the problems attached to Ehrman's skeptical conclusions, but you'll also be in a better position to respond to the objections posed by critiques of the Bible in general and equip others to do the same.

Discussion Questions

1. Had you heard of Bart Ehrman prior to reading this book? If so, are you favorably inclined toward his views? Why or why not?
2. Have you come across some of the same skeptical arguments about Christianity and the Bible Ehrman raises? If so, where, and how did you deal with those arguments?
3. What is the biggest problem you have with Christianity and the Bible? If none, what is the biggest problem your family and/or friends have?

Chapter One

IS GOD IMMORAL BECAUSE HE ALLOWS SUFFERING?

Claims Addressed

---

1. It is a contradiction to say that God is sovereign and God is good in view of all the evil in the world.

2. The Bible contains many different answers to the problem of why there is suffering in the world, and many of these answers contradict one another.

3. The Bible's explanations for suffering and evil are not satisfying.

4. The God of the Bible is immoral. Therefore, he cannot exist.

Bart Ehrman's Problem

As mentioned, Bart Ehrman is an expert in the study of ancient biblical manuscripts. He has a great deal of experience in the exploration of early Christianity, and his knowledge of the New Testament is considerable. But Ehrman is not a philosopher or a theologian. His lack of expertise in these fields becomes increasingly apparent in his book *God's Problem*, where Ehrman explains the reason he ultimately gave up on Christianity.

At times Ehrman's honesty is refreshing. He admits he sometimes wakes up at night sweating at the prospect that he is wrong and hell is real.[1] He also displays, at least for a biblical scholar, a good sense of humor (we are not normally known for this particular quality).

Also, it is commendable that Ehrman interacts so much with the biblical material. We wish popular Christian authors would learn from his example (though we hope they would take a different approach). Bart Ehrman takes the Bible seriously. He just doesn't believe most of what it says.

Though we disagree with many of Ehrman's arguments, we respect him as a man—God's image bearer—and can appreciate and even agree with some of his conclusions. When we meet, and two of us have shared events with him, the meeting is cordial and engaging. Acting in love and respect is what image bearers of God are called to do with others who bear his image.

But here is a point that should not be overlooked: though Ehrman doesn't believe in God, he has reciprocated with kindness toward us. Why? In one sense the answer is fairly simple: Ehrman has morals. You can see it in the way he argues against God's existence. For instance, he writes, "Others, of course, refuse to believe in a God who is determined to exterminate the people he created because he disapproves of how they behave."[2]

He also writes, "I came to believe that there is not a God who is intent on roasting innocent children and others in hell because they didn't happen to accept a certain religious creed."[3] Or consider what he advocates people should do in light of evil and suffering: "But we should also work hard to make our world the most pleasing place it can be *for others*. . . . What we have in the here and now is all that there is. We need to live life to its fullest and help others as well to enjoy the fruits of the land."[4]

So, according to Ehrman, we should help others. Who would want to argue with him here? But here is the problem: *Ehrman never explains, in light of his worldview, why humans should try to relieve suffering in other humans.* He makes a forceful case that

---

[1] Bart D. Ehrman, *God's Problem: How the Bible Fails to Answer Our Most Important Question—Why We Suffer* (New York: HarperCollins, 2008), 127.

[2] Ibid., 66.

[3] Ibid., 128.

[4] Ibid., 278.

the God of the Bible is wrong on account of his actions (or lack thereof) in the face of egregious evil and suffering, but he never explains the *basis* for his moral outrage.

The more Ehrman builds his case against God based on morality, and the more he urges people to help others, the more the problem surfaces: Where is Ehrman getting his morality? *Who decides what is right and wrong?* If Ehrman were to say it is up to a given society to determine its morality, it would seem to follow that when Nazi Germany decided it was right to kill millions of Jews or when a society decides it is right to abuse women or kill babies with disabilities to protect the gene pool, then these things are right, at least for these groups of people, and there is no higher court of appeal. Most will find this logic unsatisfying. In any case it is unlikely that Ehrman would make such a claim since he discusses the evils of the Holocaust.[5]

So if society does not decide what is good and what is evil, *who decides what is right and wrong?* Perhaps Ehrman might reply that right or wrong is whatever is most helpful for the majority of the human race. However, why should one who believes that this world is all we have care about the human race at large? If there is no God, and we live in a strictly material, evolving universe, violence and suffering are just part of the natural world with no inherent morality attached to them. In this case violence would not be evil; it would simply be part of the evolutionary process.

If so, why should we seek to eliminate suffering and violence? If all we are is a collection of physical matter and all we have is this life, why should Ehrman care about people he doesn't even know who are dying of AIDS in Africa? Or, for that matter, why should he care if people whom he *does* know are suffering? Those who believe in God argue that we should care because God created us to care and commanded that we love others. But without God, compassion for others is nothing but chemical changes in the brain. Suffering is meaningless. Violence is meaningless. All is meaningless![6] Ed Budziszewski describes the problem when God's existence is denied from his own personal experience:

---

[5] *God's Problem*, 91–92.

[6] Before my conversion to Christianity in my late college years, this is what I (Andreas

Everything goes wrong without God. This is true even of the good things He's given us, such as our minds. One of the good things I've been given is a stronger than average mind. . . . The problem is that a strong mind that refuses the call to serve God has its own way of going wrong. When some people flee from God they rob and kill. When others flee from God they do a lot of drugs and have a lot of sex. When I fled from God I didn't do any of those things; my way of fleeing was to get stupid. Though it always comes as a surprise to intellectuals, there are some forms of stupidity that one must be highly intelligent and educated to commit.

Paul said that the knowledge of God's law is "written on our hearts, our consciences also bearing witness." That means that as long as we have minds, *we can't not know* them. Well, I was unusually determined not to know them; therefore I had to destroy my mind. I resisted the temptation to believe in good with as much energy as some saints resist the temptation to neglect good. For instance, I loved my wife and children, but I was determined to regard this love as merely a subjective preference with no real and objective value. Think what this did to my very capacity to love them. After all, love is a commitment of the will to the true good of another person, and how can one's will be committed to the true good of another person if he denies the reality of good, denies the reality of persons, and denies that his commitments are in his control?

Visualize a man opening up the access panels of his mind and pulling out all the components that have God's image stamped on them. The

---

Köstenberger) in fact believed, following some of the great French existentialist thinkers.

problem is that they all have God's image stamped on them, so the man can never stop. No matter how much he pulls out, there's still more to pull. I was that man. Because I pulled out more and more, there was less and less that I could think about. But because there was less and less that I could think about, I thought I was becoming more and more focused. Because I believed things that filled me with dread, I thought I was smarter and braver than the people who didn't believe them. I thought I saw an emptiness at the heart of the universe that was hidden from their foolish eyes. Of course I was the fool.[7]

Without God, Ehrman has no grounding for his morality. What is more, if one responds to the question, "Who decides what is right and wrong?" with "Right is what is most helpful to the human race," this only leads to something akin to the initial question. After all, what is most helpful for the human race? Hitler and a whole list of others would disagree with Ehrman on what is best for the human race. Is the murder of old people good for the human race as a whole? Is the killing of children with disabilities good for the human race in general?

So we are back to the question: *Who decides what is right and wrong?* Apparently, at least in his world, Ehrman himself gets to decide what is right and wrong. And Ehrman ultimately decides that God's got a problem! But Ehrman has never told us where he gets his notion of right and wrong. Regardless of whether God has a problem, one thing is clear: Bart Ehrman has a problem. Without God, Ehrman has no legitimate or sufficient basis for his morality.

---

[7] Ed Budziszewski, "Escape from Nihilism," *re:generation Quarterly* 4, no. 1 (1998): 13–14; cf. D. A. Carson, *The God Who Is There: Finding Your Place in God's Story* (Wheaton: Crossway, 2010), 173.

God, Evil, and Suffering

Claim 1: *It is a contradiction to say that God is sovereign and God is good in view of all the evil in the world.*

In the past this argument has frequently been made against Christianity. However, most philosophers, both religious and secular, now recognize that while there is a mystery in the relationship between God and evil, no internal dilemma threatens the rationality of the belief in God.[8] This is the case for primarily two reasons.

First, the argument against God's sovereignty and goodness in the face of all the evil in the world is self-contradictory because it assumes an absolute moral framework that is inconsistent with a worldview in which God is absent. Alister McGrath explains:

> Some atheists argue that the existence of suffering is evil and therefore is in itself adequate to disprove the existence of God. This is a curious argument, since closer examination shows that it is self-defeating. An argument from the existence of evil to non-existence of God depends on establishing that suffering is indeed evil. But this is not an empirical observation—it is a moral judgment. Suffering is natural; for it to be evil, a moral framework has to be presupposed. But where does this framework come from? The argument requires the existence of an absolute moral framework if it is to work. Yet the existence of such an absolute framework is itself widely seen as pointing to God's existence. In the end, the nonexistence of God seems to end up depending on God's existence. It's not the best argument. Yet if it's simply my personal perception that nature

---

[8] "At present however, it is widely conceded that there is nothing like straightforward contradiction or necessary falsehood in the joint affirmation of God and evil; the existence of evil is not logically incompatible (even in the broadly logical sense) with the existence of an all-powerful, all-knowing, and perfectly good God." Alvin Plantinga, *Warranted Christian Belief* (Oxford: Oxford University Press, 2000), 461.

is evil, this has no relevance to the debate about God. It might simply say something about my naïve and sentimental tastes rather than about the deeper structure of the universe.[9]

Second, this argument assumes a "God's eye view." The problem is, of course, that no human has a "God's eye view." Ehrman says he can't think of satisfying reasons suffering exists, so there must not be a good reason; thus, there must not be a God. But just because Ehrman (or any other person, for that matter) can't understand why God would allow suffering, does this mean God doesn't exist? Only if Ehrman has a "God's eye view" will he legitimately be able to say that because he doesn't see any good reason for certain (or all) forms of suffering, there must not be one. Tim Keller summarizes Alvin Plantinga's illustration of "no-see-ums" to provide a helpful analogy at this point:

> If you look into your pup tent for a St. Bernard, and you don't see one, it is reasonable to assume that there is no St. Bernard in your tent. But if you look into your pup tent for a "no-see-um" (an extremely small insect with a bite out of all proportion to its size) and you don't see any, it is not reasonable to assume they aren't there. Because, after all, no one can see 'em. Many assume that if there were good reasons for the existence of evil, they would be accessible to our minds, more like St. Bernards than like no-see-ums, but why should that be the case?[10]

---

[9] Alister E. McGrath, *Mere Apologetics: How to Help Seekers and Skeptics Find Faith* (Grand Rapids: Baker, 2012), 163–64. Alvin Plantinga comes to the same conclusion: "Accordingly, if you think there really is such a thing as horrifying wickedness (that our sense that there is, is not a mere illusion of some sort), and if you also think the main options are theism and naturaliksm, then you have a powerful theistic argument for evil." Alvin Plantinga, "A Christian Life Partly Lived," in *Philosophers Who Believe: The Spiritual Journeys of 11 Leading Thinkers*, ed. Kelly James Clark (Downers Grove: InterVarsity, 1997), 73.

[10] Timothy Keller, *The Reason for God: Conversations on Faith and Life* (New York: Dutton, 2010), 24.

Ehrman admits that the biblical authors remind us that suffering and evil can be a mystery we as humans cannot fully understand. Yet the Bible calls on us to accept that at times an infinite God cannot be fully understood by finite beings and to trust in a God who does fully understand. Ehrman seems to agree that suffering is something we cannot fully understand but then makes the giant leap to say that if *he* cannot understand, there must not be an explanation. This is poor logic; one argument simply doesn't follow from the other.

For these two reasons most philosophers, even those who claim atheism, agree that suffering in this world is not a convincing argument against belief in the existence of God. Surprisingly, in his book on the subject, Ehrman never addresses either of these two reasons, though one doesn't have to search long to find such explanations in the relevant literature. The irony here is striking: in a book entitled *God's Problem*, Ehrman doesn't interact with the major problems set against his own position.

Claim 2:   *The Bible contains many different answers to the problem of why there is suffering in the world, and many of these answers contradict one another.*

In *God's Problem*, Ehrman surveys the Bible's various books and genres in search of their explanations of suffering. He finds the Bible offers five major explanations:

- *Suffering comes from God as a punishment against sin.* He calls this the classical view.
- *Suffering is the result of human beings sinning against other human beings.* Ehrman mentions that this is related to the notion that humans have free will and are able to make decisions, even if this is damaging to themselves and others.
- *Suffering is redemptive.* In other words, suffering exists in order for God to bring about a good that would not have been possible without the evil.
- *Suffering is a test of faith.* God uses suffering to see who will serve him and believe in him despite their circumstances.

- *Suffering at times is mysterious.* Many times God doesn't give us the exact reason we suffer but expects us to trust him.

According to Ehrman, many of these explanations are contradictory. But it is difficult to understand why he thinks any of these answers are necessarily at odds with one another. Ehrman is quick to claim there are contradictions in the Bible, as we'll see in subsequent chapters, but he never really defends why he sees these various explanations as contradictory. Yes, different biblical authors at times focus on a given explanation, but this doesn't mean they thought they were providing *the* universal answer to suffering and evil that must be applied to every situation. Even Ehrman seems to admit this: "The prophets and other biblical writers, of course, were not stating a general religious principle that was to be accepted as true for all times and places. They were speaking to a specific time and place."[11]

Nevertheless, Ehrman at times seems to ignore his own statement. For example, he admits that he can see where *some* suffering is redemptive. He tells the story of how becoming sick and being held out of sports for a season as a teenager helped lay a foundation for his career in academic research. Yet he then argues that not *all* suffering is redemptive. One has to wonder against whom he is arguing at this point. After all, the Bible would agree with him. *Some* suffering is for *other* reasons, such as punishment for sin. Also, many times in particular instances, we can't understand why suffering is taking place. It could be for one of the explanations offered in the above list or for another reason of which we are unaware. Claiming that there are explanations for suffering is different from saying we'll know what the explanation is in every situation.

Only if one assumes that each biblical author was giving an exhaustive explanation for suffering (which Ehrman himself seems to admit is not the case) and fails to read the Bible as a whole can one argue that the biblical explanations for evil and suffering are contradictory. Since he gives little attention to explaining why he believes these explanations are contradictory, the real problem for

---

[11] Ehrman, *God's Problem*, 90.

Ehrman is *not* that there are *contradictory explanations* but that he *doesn't like the Bible's explanations*. This leads to our next response.

Claim 3: *The Bible's explanations for suffering and evil are not satisfying.*

Ehrman doesn't deny that the Bible provides explanations for evil and suffering (see the list of explanations he provides in the response to claim 2 above); he just doesn't care for the explanations it gives. Several responses to Ehrman are in order at this point.

First, the ultimate test for the Bible's truthfulness can never be based on whether certain people like its answers. If the IRS calls me tomorrow to tell me that I made a mistake and need to pay more taxes, I won't like the information. I might protest that I've already paid enough taxes; but if the IRS says I owe more, my dislike for what they're saying makes little difference in whether their claim is true. God doesn't cease to exist just because Bart Ehrman doesn't like the answers God has given.

Second, often Ehrman wrongly casts the biblical explanations as absolutes that must apply to every situation and then mocks the position for not corresponding to reality. For instance, consider his evaluation of the classical view:

> The problem with this view is not only that it is scandalous and outrageous, but also that it creates both false security and false guilt. If punishment comes because of sin, and I'm not suffering one bit, thank you very much, does that make me righteous? More righteous than my next door neighbor who lost his job, or whose child was killed in an accident, or whose wife was brutally raped and murdered? On the other hand, if I am undergoing intense suffering, is it really because God is punishing me? Am I really to blame when my child is born with a defect? When the economy takes a nosedive and I can no longer put food on the table? When I get cancer?[12]

---

[12] Ibid., 55.

Only by disconnecting the classical view from the multifaceted biblical explanation of suffering can Ehrman make the classical view look silly. The Bible does not insist that punishment is the *only* reason people suffer. In fact, one only has to read the Old Testament book of Job to see how this simplistic view of suffering is corrected in Scripture. Or one might look at Jesus' response when his disciples ask him whether a man was born blind because of his sin or that of his parents. Apparently the question stemmed from the implied assumption that there is a direct cause-and-effect relationship between suffering and sin in all circumstances. Jesus replied, "Neither this man nor his parents sinned" (John 9:3). By saying this, Jesus was not disavowing the classical view. At other times, Jesus accepted that individual suffering can be linked to specific sins (John 5:14; cf. Luke 13:2–3), and he certainly affirmed that in a general sense all suffering is a result of the fall (Genesis 3). Ironically, analogous to Jesus' first disciples, Ehrman is guilty of evaluating the various biblical explanations independent from the larger biblical framework the Scriptures provide.

Third, Ehrman heavily critiques, even mocks, the Christian position for saying that suffering and evil are at times a mystery but then turns around to offer no alternative explanation of his own other than to say, "All that is here is all that we have." For instance, Ehrman writes, "At the end of the day, one would have to say that the answer is a mystery. . . . And this presents a problem, because if in the end the question is resolved by saying it is a mystery, then it is no longer an answer. It is an admission that there is no answer."[13] It is surprising that Ehrman, as an agnostic, doesn't want to allow Christians to offer as one of their responses to suffering and evil that finite beings cannot fully understand the ways of an infinite God. Ironically, Ehrman admits that he has no real explanation from his worldview either but nonetheless insists that the Christian claim of mystery as one of the multifaceted responses to evil is a "copout."

---

[13] Ibid., 13.

The fact is that suffering and evil are a mystery no matter what perspective one adopts. Alister McGrath puts it well when he writes,

> Ultimately this is a question that *nobody*— whether secular or religious—can answer totally. The real issue is who can offer the most existential satisfying answer, which stands up to critical reflection despite leaving some questions unanswered—perhaps because, given our human limitations, they are ultimately unanswerable. A willingness to live with irresolvable questions is a mark of intellectual maturity, not a matter of logical nonsense as some unwisely regard it.[14]

Perhaps this is why Ehrman remains an agnostic: he knows there are unanswerable questions in any worldview, and fundamentalists (in keeping with his religious roots) don't want questions; they want pat answers. Yet no matter the explanation, some questions still remain, so no one view will ever completely satisfy him.

The Bible offers a variety of answers that have powerful explanatory value, but these answers are not exhaustive. The list of biblical explanations taken from Ehrman's *God's Problem* (see claim 2 in this chapter for the list) gives us part of the picture. Scripture gives true answers, yes; but the Bible doesn't tell us everything we would like to know. Assuming there is a God who stands behind the Bible, why would he be under obligation to explain everything? Apparently, Ehrman assumes that for God to be real, he must produce exhaustive answers to all of Ehrman's questions. We've seen that Ehrman has set up his own criteria for evaluating God: for God to be real, he must offer explanations that Ehrman likes and that are exhaustive. But is this reasonable? Hardly. It is neither logical nor rational.

Fourth, Ehrman fails to recognize the powerful impact the Christian doctrine of the incarnation has on the discussion of evil

---

[14] McGrath, *Mere Apologetics*, 166–67.

and suffering. The New Testament teaches that God entered the world and suffered alongside, and even on behalf of, his people (John 1:1–2, 14; Phil 2:5–7; Heb 4:14–15). No matter the trial, the suffering, or the evil facing humans, they must never assume God doesn't care. Alvin Plantinga explains that if this were not true,

> it would be easy to see God as remote and detached, permitting all these evils, himself untouched, in order to achieve ends that are no doubt exalted but have little to do with us, and little power to assuage our griefs. It would be easy to see him as cold and unfeeling—or if loving, then such that his love for us has little to do with our perception of our own welfare. But God, as Christians see him, is neither remote nor detached. His aims and goals may be beyond our ken and may require our suffering, but he is himself prepared to accept much greater suffering in the pursuit of those ends.[15]

While the incarnation doesn't explain the *theoretical* problem of evil, it does provide a powerful resource in response to the *existential* problem of evil.[16]

Finally, much of Ehrman's dissatisfaction with the Bible's explanation of suffering is bound up with the concern that, for him, God appears to act immorally. Since this accusation against God can in some ways stand alone as a separate argument, it deserves more attention. We'll turn to this in the next section where we'll once again see some major problems in Ehrman's reasoning.

---

[15] Plantinga, "A Christian Life Partly Lived," 72.

[16] Tim Keller makes a compelling case that Christianity, compared to the other major worldviews, offers the best resources to cope with suffering. See Tim Keller, *Walking with God through Pain and Suffering* (New York: Dutton, 2005), esp. chaps. 1–3. He concludes that secularism "is probably the weakest of all worldviews at helping its adherents understand and endure the 'terror of life'" (p. 86).

Claim 4:   *The God of the Bible is immoral.*
             Therefore, he cannot exist.

Once again, Ehrman's argument undercuts itself. This has been
noted in several of the previous responses, but it's worth summarizing what has already been noted. Without God, Ehrman has no
way of distinguishing morality from immorality; and, remarkably,
his objections to God based on morality actually provide a powerful argument for God. Tim Keller makes this point well:

> Modern day objections to God [that are based
> on evil in the world] are based on a sense of fair
> play and justice. People, we believe, ought not to
> suffer, be excluded, die of hunger or oppression.
> But the evolutionary mechanism of natural selec-
> tion *depends* on death, destruction, and violence
> of the strong against the weak—these things are
> all perfectly natural. On what basis, then, does
> the atheist judge the natural world to be horri-
> bly wrong, unfair, and unjust? The nonbeliever in
> God doesn't have a good basis for being outraged
> at injustice. . . . If you are *sure* that this natural
> world is unjust and filled with evil, you are assum-
> ing the reality of some extra-natural (or supernat-
> ural) standard by which to make your judgment.[17]

What is more, many of Ehrman's problems with the God of
the Bible can be traced to the fact that he persistently refuses to
see God as having divine rights over his creation and the evil of
humans in their rebellion against their Creator. Ehrman might
respond that he no longer believes these truths, which is why he
has refused to accept them in his evaluation of the biblical explanations. However, even if one refuses to believe in God or the
Bible, one must be willing to approach the biblical explanations of
suffering with the Bible's larger framework in mind.

For example, imagine someone is trying to argue the legitimacy of naturalistic evolution to a person who responds in the

---

[17] Keller, *The Reason for God*, 26.

following way: "Well, that just can't be the case because the Bible doesn't say that." Assuming the person explaining naturalistic evolution has no loyalty to the Bible, it does little good for the other person to respond in this way. In order to understand naturalistic evolution, one must be willing to hypothetically suspend belief in God in order to understand the alternate worldview and evaluate its coherency. In other words, one must be willing, at least initially, to engage a worldview on *its* terms, not one's own. This is where Ehrman falters. He fails to engage the Christian worldview on its own terms and thus finds the Bible's presentation of God lacking.

First, Ehrman consistently maintains that God doesn't have the right to do certain things. He implies that God has no right to judge, to punish, or to destroy. But if God is God, the Creator of all things and the One who stands above all things, then it is difficult to argue that God is wrong when he acts the way he does. This is never more evident than when Ehrman displays his outrage at the notion of divine judgment. Ehrman, of course, is not alone in his disdain for a God who would send anyone to hell; it is surely one of Christianity's most offensive doctrines.

Tim Keller writes of a discussion he had with a woman who shared Ehrman's outrage concerning a judging God. Keller recounts the conversation:

> "Why are you offended by the idea of a forgiving God?" She looked puzzled. I continued, "I respectfully urge you to consider your cultural location when you find the Christian teaching about hell offensive." I went on to point out that secular Westerners get upset by the Christian doctrine of hell, but they find Biblical teaching about turning the other cheek and forgiving enemies appealing. I then asked her to consider how someone from a very different culture sees Christianity. In traditional societies the teaching about "turning the other cheek" makes absolutely no sense. It offends people's deepest instincts about what is right. For

them the doctrine of a God of judgment, however,
is no problem at all.[18]

Keller concluded the conversation by asking, "Why should cultural sensibilities be the final court in which to judge where Christianity is valid?"[19] Ehrman and contemporary culture might not like the idea that God, for a variety of reasons (some of which are not fully known to us), punishes people or allows suffering. Nevertheless, their disdain for suffering doesn't obviate the existence of God any more than another culture's disdain for the doctrine of divine forgiveness means Christianity is false.

Second, Ehrman's outrage against what he sees as the immoral actions of the God of the Bible is rooted in his denial of the biblical doctrine of sin.[20] Ehrman underestimates the majesty of God; and despite the lists of evils in the world, he also unduly minimizes the sheer evil of humanity's rebellion against God as taught in Scripture. Ehrman's understanding of evil is limited to the horizontal level, people perpetrating evil toward other human beings. The Bible affirms the *horizontal* nature of evil but claims the *root* of evil is *vertical*; that is, evil acts are in the final analysis rebellion against God. According to the Bible, ultimately all horizontal offenses are vertical offenses against God. When people lie or steal or mistreat others, they sin first and foremost against God (Ps 51:1–7). This is not only because he is the Creator but also because it is God and his standard against which people rebel.

The difference between Ehrman and the Bible shouldn't be overlooked. For Ehrman, evil is evil because it hurts other people. According to the Bible, people hurting others for no legitimate

---

[18] Ibid., 74.

[19] Ibid., 74–75.

[20] For more on how to understand the passages in the Old Testament where God judges nations (and even the nation of Israel) through warfare, see Heath A. Thomas, Jeremy Evans, and Paul Copan, eds., *Holy War in the Bible: Christian Morality and an Old Testament Problem* (Downers Grove: IVP, 2013), which is a collection of essays from different academic specialists. Also see Paul Copan, *Is God a Moral Monster? Making Sense of the Old Testament God* (Grand Rapids: Baker, 2011); and for more concise treatments see G.K. Beale, *The Morality of God in the Old Testament* (Phillipsburg, NJ: P&R, 2013) and the section titled "Was the Slaughter of Canaanites an Act of 'Divine Genocide'?," in William Lane Craig and Joseph E. Gorra, *A Reasonable Response: Answers to Tough Questions on God, Christianity, and the Bible* (Chicago: Moody, 2013), 275–84.

reason is evil, but this is only *part* of what makes evil so intolerable. According to the Bible, evil is evil *because it offends a holy and righteous God.* The magnitude of this offense is difficult for humans to imagine, especially in this day and age when personal accountability is in increasingly short supply. We don't like anyone telling us what to do. But the Bible teaches that, in a general sense, all suffering is rooted in cosmic rebellion against a God who tried to tell us what to do. How dare he? Due to this rebellion the good and perfect world God created descended in a downward spiral. Because we all, not only corporately but also individually, are part of this rebellion, we approach the question of God and his role in human suffering with the notion that we are undeserving of this evil world. Yet the Bible sees things in view of the cosmic rebellion and insists that God graciously gives good things to the world *despite our evil.* From this perspective perhaps it would be more appropriate to speak of the "problem of good": in view of all our individual and corporate evil, how is it that God, in his love, gives us so many of the *good* things we enjoy in this world?

While the Bible teaches that all people have turned away from their Creator, it doesn't deny that there are "good" people. Christian theologians have long pointed out that not all people, comparatively speaking, are equally "good" or "bad." There is a difference between Adolf Hitler and Mother Teresa or between Osama bin Laden and Billy Graham. Normally, when considering the question, "How can bad things happen to good people?" this is the type of comparative good or bad most have in mind. Indeed, the Bible asks the question at times in a similar way (consider the book of Job). But, though this is no doubt an unpopular notion, it is also important to accept that the Bible also teaches that, at a deeper level, we have *all* slapped God in the face, shaken our fists in rebellion against him, and told our Creator that we would do things *our way* (Rom 3:9–20).[21] In view of God's righteousness and holiness, what is shocking is that God didn't respond with immediate justice. Instead, his merciful plan was to enter into his

---

[21] In keeping with the old Frank Sinatra song "My Way."

creation in the person of his Son in order to make things right and
to overcome the evil of his creatures (Rom 5:8).

Ehrman, a Believer?

Without God Ehrman has nothing in which to ground the
morality that undergirds the premise of his arguments. He has nothing but the deep-seated feeling that this world is not as it should
be. The Bible says that all humans—God's image bearers—have his
morality stamped on their souls, though this morality can be suppressed in various ways. Ehrman's stories and statistics of horrible
suffering and evil that he provides in *God's Problem* serve to remind
us of what we know from various experiences all too well: something
has gone terribly wrong. Of course, the Bible tells us exactly what
happened. But Ehrman no longer believes the Bible. Nevertheless, he
is still a believer, at least in much of the Bible's standard for morality.
Ehrman can't escape the Bible's morality because it is written on his
heart by the same One who stands behind the Bible he now rejects.
Perhaps for Ehrman, as McGrath has written, "[t]his is a matter of
the heart, rather than the head." McGrath continues,

> Where does this deep-seated intuition that suffer-
> ing and pain are not right come from? . . . What if
> this intuition points to something deeper—some-
> thing built into us that reflects our true nature and
> identity? What if this revulsion against suffering
> and pain is a reminder of paradise, on one hand,
> and an anticipation of the New Jerusalem on the
> other? What if our thoughts about the present
> state of things are shaped by our intuitive realiza-
> tion of our true origins and destiny?[22]

Despite these intuitions that point to something greater,
Ehrman ultimately says that if the God of the Bible did exist, he
would be responsible for the evil in the world. Instead, the Bible
says that suffering entered the world because *God's creatures
rebelled*. Despite this rebellion God entered into his creation to

---

[22] McGrath, *Mere Apologetics*, 166.

remind his creatures that he not only cares enough to suffer with us, but he also cares enough to establish a plan to make this world right again. The Bible does not glibly answer the question of evil and suffering by saying such things as that, with enough human effort, "there does not have to be world poverty."[23] The Bible takes evil and suffering far too seriously to offer such a simplistic and naïve response.

Indeed, God wants humanity to serve him and seek to make this world a better place, but the Bible insists that no one other than the Creator himself will ultimately make things right again. Despite a worldview that cannot justify his intuition that this world is not as it should be, Ehrman's intuition points to the Christian expectation that one day God *will* make things as they should be. We are reminded of this expectation, which has for the last 2,000 years given Christians a remarkable amount of courage and hope in times of tragedy, in some of the closing words of the book of Revelation: "Then I saw a new heaven and a new earth, for the first heaven and the first earth had passed away. . . . He will wipe away every tear from their eyes. Death will no longer exist; grief, crying, and pain will exist no longer, because the previous things have passed away" (Rev 21:1, 4).[24]

Discussion Questions

1. Describe how one might ground a moral code without God. What are the problems with trying to do this?
2. What complications arise when humans charge God with injustice?
3. What are some of the various explanations the Bible gives for suffering? Do you find these contradictory? Explain why or why not.

---

[23] Ehrman, *God's Problem*, 276. For a recent constructive Christian engagement with world poverty, see Wayne Grudem and Barry Asmus, *The Poverty of Nations: A Sustainable Solution* (Wheaton: Crossway, 2013).

[24] For more on this subject of God and suffering, see Keller, *Walking with God through Pain and Suffering*; D. A. Carson, *How Long, O Lord? Reflections on Suffering and Evil*, 2nd ed. (Grand Rapids: Baker, 2006); and Christopher W. Morgan and Robert A. Peterson, *Suffering and the Goodness of God* (Wheaton: Crossway, 2008).

4. How does the Christian theology of the incarnation and the cross provide hope in the midst of suffering and evil?

Chapter Two

IS THE BIBLE FULL OF IRRESOLVABLE CONTRADICTIONS?

Claims Addressed
---

1. The New Testament authors have contradictory points of view on major issues.

2. Attempts to reconcile various events in the New Testament are mistaken because such harmonizations create another account that is different from the ones being read.

3. The Gospels' chronological differences are historical contradictions.

4. The Gospels are so different in detail that they must be deemed in error at numerous points and cannot be viewed as divinely inspired.

5. The diversity of views within the New Testament indicates that "Jesus was not originally considered to be God in any sense at all. . . . he eventually became divine for his followers in some sense before he came to be thought of as equal with God Almighty in an absolute sense."

Bart Ehrman, Fundamentalist?

As Jesus pointed out, and Abraham Lincoln famously repeated, "A house divided against itself cannot stand."[1] Bart Ehrman is smart enough to know that if he can show that

---
[1] See Matt 12:25 and parallels. Abraham Lincoln quoted Jesus' statement with reference to the issue of slavery in his famous Gettysburg Address.

the Bible is full of contradictions, this will significantly weaken its appeal and authority. Throughout Ehrman's writings, he regularly cites the "modern scholarly consensus" in support of his claims. According to Ehrman, his views are "standard fare," held by "all my closest friends," are "widely accepted among New Testament scholars," and are "widely taught in seminaries and divinity schools."[2] However, it is only by defining scholarship on his own terms and by excluding scholars who disagree with him that Ehrman is able to imply that he is supported by all other scholarship. As one recent reviewer of Ehrman has noted,

> He fails to mention that of all the ATS-accredited seminaries in the United States, the top ten largest seminaries are all evangelical. These seminaries represent thousands and thousands of students, and hundreds and hundreds of professors. If virtually all seminary professors agree with Ehrman, then who are these professors teaching at the ten largest US seminaries? Apparently the only schools that count in Ehrman's analysis of modern seminaries are the ones that already agree with him. It is not so difficult to prove your views are mainstream when you get to decide what is mainstream.[3]

It appears that Ehrman's rhetoric is designed to intimidate a lay audience. Often his comments force readers into accepting his assertion by the mere weight of the unanimity in his circle of scholarship, which he makes out to be the only real type of scholarship. While this argument might give Ehrman a psychological edge with some readers, it proves unhelpful in dealing with the actual evidence.

---

[2] Bart D. Ehrman, *Jesus, Interrupted: Revealing the Hidden Contradictions in the Bible (And Why We Don't Know About Them)* (San Francisco: HarperOne, 2009), 17–18, 271.
[3] Michael J. Kruger, "Review of *Jesus, Interrupted*," accessed April 25, 2012, http://www.reformation21.org/shelf-life/jesus-interrupted.php. ATS (the Association of Theological Schools) is the agency that accredits many seminaries in the United States.

Even when he occasionally mentions that conservative scholars disagree, he says something like, "Scholars today, outside the
ranks of fundamentalists and conservative evangelicals, are virtually unified."[4] The problem with this type of argument is that it is
kind of like saying, "Everyone in the government, except for conservatives or Republicans, wants to raise taxes." Technically, the
statement may be accurate, but the problem is that once you qual-
ify "everyone" with "except for conservatives and Republicans,"
you are down to about half of America's elected officials. In other
words, saying that all scholarship agrees with him on a particular
point means very little since he gets to define what he means by
"scholarship."

The fact is that hundreds of reputable biblical scholars disagree with Ehrman on his key points. For example, consider Ben
Witherington's remarks:

> What is interesting is that the more I studied the
> Bible the less I was prone to accuse the Bible of
> obvious historical errors and stupid mistakes,
> including theological errors about a matter as
> profound as human suffering and evil. To the con-
> trary, I found the Bible rich, complex, varied, and
> helpful and truthful in dealing with precisely such
> life and death matters. It would be appropriate
> then to ask—why exactly did studying the Bible
> in the same way at seminary and during doctoral
> work lead Bart Ehrman and myself to such differ-
> ent conclusions? In my case, my faith in the Bible
> was strengthened, but the opposite seems to have
> been the case with Bart. "This is a mystery and it
> calls for profound reflection." Some of this clearly
> has to do with presuppositions.[5]

[4] Bart D. Ehrman, *Did Jesus Exist? The Historical Argument for Jesus of Nazareth* (San Francisco: HarperOne, 2013), 47.

[5] Ben Witherington III, "Bart Interrupted," accessed March 25, 2010, http://benwitherington.
blogspot.com/2009/04/bart-interrupted-part-four.html.

Witherington and Ehrman are both New Testament scholars who have published dozens of serious peer-reviewed articles
and monographs. Both have spent their adult lives in serious academic study of the Bible and other ancient literature. Yet as Ben
Witherington has pointed out, despite their similarities, he and
Ehrman have very different views on the reliability of the New
Testament. This, at least in part, has to do with presuppositions.

Though Ehrman has gone on a journey from fundamentalist
all the way to an "agnostic with atheist leanings," ironically many
of his presuppositions about what the New Testament must be
to be divinely inspired have remained unchanged.[6] He held and
seems to still hold that for the New Testament to be inspired, it
must have certain characteristics. (1) It must have been copied a
certain way throughout the years. (2) One must have close to absolute certainty about virtually every reading and translation. And,
apparently, (3) the Bible must contain books that say the same
things in almost exactly the same way. When Ehrman realized
the Bible didn't meet his expectations, he fell, and he fell hard. He
began to see diversity as contradictions. He began to see legitimate
development within the Bible as irreconcilable differences. He
began to view harmonization as irresponsible history. The Bible
could no longer fit Ehrman's rigid categories of what he thought
it was; therefore, he no longer deemed it reliable or inspired at all.
Ironically, Ehrman's fundamentalist presuppositions of what the
Bible must be to be divinely inspired seem not to have changed
much, though his view concerning the Bible's actual ability to live
up to such standards has clearly changed.

Despite Ehrman's objections, one of the remarkable characteristics of the New Testament documents and their various authors
is that they offer a rich picture of Jesus, salvation, and the Christian
life, which in all its diversity is unified around a cluster of central
themes and culminates the salvation-historical story narrated in
the Old Testament.

First, it has been demonstrated that there are at least three inte-
grative motifs found in the writings of all the major New Testament

---

[6] Ibid., 5.

authors, which are also foundational beliefs of Jesus and the early church. (1) There is one God. (2) Jesus is the Messiah and exalted Lord. (3) The Christian community has been entrusted with the proclamation of the gospel.[7] There are many other common themes, but these are three of the major pillars in the theology of the New Testament. With these pillars in mind, "The question we must ask is not whether these books all say the same thing, but whether they all bear witness to the same Jesus and through him to the many splendoured wisdom of the one true God."[8]

Second, the New Testament is unified in picking up the story narrated in the Hebrew Scriptures (i.e., the Old Testament). These Scriptures bear witness to a God who created a good world and humans as the pinnacle of his creation. However, people turned away from God and fell into sin. Judgment ensued, and the entire creation was negatively affected. Ever since, things have not been as they should be. Yet God, in his mercy, chose to bless and restore the world through the nation of Israel. God made a covenant with Israel and, despite the nation's repeated unfaithfulness, remained faithful to his promises. As part of these covenant commitments, God promised to raise up a king like David to rule forever and be a blessing to the world. The New Testament picks up this story and proclaims Jesus as this Davidic king who blessed the world through his life, death, and resurrection and who will return at the end of time to restore all of creation. The New Testament's unity does not consist in retelling the story in identical terms over and over again. Instead, it weaves together diverse scenes, events, genres, and perspectives in its presentation of Jesus' first and second coming and the implications of his ministry for believers and the world.

The early church, for its part, viewed the diversity of the New Testament documents as an advantage rather than a liability. They did not get rid of the four Gospels in order to enshrine one Gospel as the exclusive witness to the events surrounding Jesus' coming. The early church understood that four historical sources are better than one because they give a richer picture of Jesus than any

---

[7] Andreas J. Köstenberger, "Diversity and Unity in the New Testament," in *Biblical Theology: Retrospect and Prospect*, ed. Scott J. Hafemann (Downers Grove: InterVarsity, 2002), 154–58.

[8] G. B. Caird, *New Testament Theology*, ed. L. D. Hurst (Oxford: Clarendon, 1994), 24.

one source could, no matter how detailed. Yes, there is legitimate diversity in the New Testament, but we must be careful to distinguish between diversity and disagreement. To be sure, the New Testament presents varied historical perspectives that at times call for harmonization. But as the response to claim 2 below will show, harmonizing parallel accounts is part of the common, ordinary role of any historian.

Does the Bible Contradict Itself?

Claim 1:   *The New Testament authors have contradictory points of view on major issues.*

Bart Ehrman explains his approach to understanding the various perspectives found in the New Testament:

> The historical-critical method maintains that we are in danger of misreading a book if we fail to let its author speak for himself, if we force his message to be exactly the same as another author's message, if we insist on reading all the books of the New Testament as one book instead of as twenty-seven books. These books were written in different times and places, under different circumstances, to address different issues; they were written by different authors with different perspectives, beliefs, assumptions, traditions, and sources. And they sometimes present different points of view on major issues.[9]

One wonders if Ehrman realizes that many conservative scholars have long been saying the same some sort of thing but without viewing it as a threat to the cogency of the New Testament. In fact, Ehrman in many ways sounds remarkably similar to the conservative evangelical scholar Craig Blomberg who writes,

---

[9] Ehrman, *Jesus, Interrupted*, 64.

In the midst of Scripture's unity, we must not lose
sight of its diversity. This takes several forms. The
books of the Bible are written by different authors,
in different times and places, to different audiences in distinct circumstances, using various
literary genres. Each book thus displays unique
purposes and themes. In some instances, different
portions of Scripture are so closely parallel that
we can postulate a literary relationship between
them and assume that their differences are intentional: sometimes theologically motivated; sometimes merely for stylistic variation.[10]

Both Ehrman and Blomberg appear to be saying similar things,
yet their tones and ultimate conclusions are in stark contrast.[11] The
difference between Ehrman and Blomberg seems bound up more
in the presuppositions that they bring to the interpretive process
rather than in the refusal, on the part of either scholar, to recognize diversity. Both argue that the different writers have diverse
theological emphases and should be allowed to speak for themselves. However, based on their witness to the same core truths,
Blomberg sees the New Testament documents as expressing different yet compatible theologies. Ehrman, maintaining a thorough-
going skepticism, fails to see any unifying core beliefs and views
these differences as contradictions.

We regularly experience life's events in different ways than our
wives do. Sometimes, in social situations, they will begin recounting an experience but at some point we will ask if we can finish the
story. It's not that our wives have a problem with honesty, so we
don't ask to tell the rest of the story because we think them in danger of getting some of the details wrong or of embellishing the story
for greater effect. Instead, we want to emphasize certain aspects of
the account, add particular details, or include something we think
that our audience would want to hear that our spouses will likely

---

[10] Craig L. Blomberg, "Unity and Diversity," in *New Dictionary of Biblical Theology*, ed. T. Des-
mond Alexander and Brian S. Rosner (Downers Grove: InterVarsity, 2000), 69–70.

[11] See Craig L. Blomberg, *Can We Still Believe the Bible? An Evangelical Engagement with
Contemporary Questions* (Grand Rapids: Brazos, 2014).

not communicate in their way of telling a story. Though the event we experienced is the same, we are different people, and as such we communicate stories differently, though not necessarily less truthfully. Again, to reduce all (or even most) diversity to contradiction is more characteristic of the type of monochrome, black-and-white fundamentalism Ehrman professes to have left behind than of the kind of judicious, nuanced scholarship to which he professes allegiance. Recognizing the unity of the New Testament does not in any way preclude the realization that the biblical authors were real people writing with particular points of view and aspects of the story they wanted to emphasize.

But suppose someone heard one of our wives tell her version of the same story and had a personal vendetta against us or her. They could possibly say, "Hey, I heard your wife tell that story differently last week; one of you is lying." Of course, on one (woodenly literal) level they would be right: the two stories would be different. But only someone who was dead set on casting all differences as contradictions would accuse one or both of us of lying. In response to such an accusation, a friend or a fair-minded acquaintance would want to slow down to hear both stories to see if such differences really meant we were contradicting each other. The New Testament authors deserve the same kind of fair-minded assessment. Unfortunately, Ehrman regularly fails to award the New Testament documents the fair and balanced treatment they deserve. The following test cases demonstrate that the alleged theological contradictions offered by Ehrman regularly turn out to be different, but not contradictory, in nature.

Test Case 1: *Mark and Luke have different depictions of the crucifixion. In Mark, Jesus dies in despair and is unsure of what is going on while, in Luke, Jesus is in complete control.*

Many scholars acknowledge that Mark and Luke offer different perspectives on Jesus' life and, as Ehrman has pointed out, also his death. The central questions appear to be whether it is illegitimate for two authors to highlight different aspects of Jesus' death and whether these different aspects are incompatible.[12]

First, the Gospel writers never claim to give an exhaustive account of all the things that happened on the cross. The Gospels indicate that Jesus was on the cross for three or more hours, which we can assume were filled with various events. Each evangelist was free to pick and choose from the various details from that day. For example, Ehrman stresses Jesus' cry in Mark, "My God, My God, why have You forsaken Me?" (Mark 15:34) in contrast to Luke 23:46, where Jesus, while on the cross, says, "Father, into Your hands I entrust My spirit." Yet Mark also indicates that Jesus let out a second cry (Mark 15:37). In addition, the four canonical Gospels provide other details and utterances by Jesus, adding up to the famous "Seven Words of Jesus at the Cross."[13] It is reasonable to assume that Jesus experienced a series of diverse emotions as he died on the cross.

A closer look at Luke's version shows something interesting in relationship to Mark. Mark tells us that Jesus cried out a second time while on the cross; however, Mark does not tell us what Jesus said then. Luke has the text from Psalm 31:5 at the very spot Mark has a second but unspecified cry from Jesus. Now most scholars see Luke as using and knowing Mark. So it is not at all unreasonable to see Luke supplying a detail Mark lacked.

Second, while it is true that Luke emphasizes Jesus' control of the situation more than Mark does, Ehrman plays up the difference for more than it's worth. Ehrman claims that Jesus, in Mark, dies in so much agony and despair that he is unsure of the reason for his death. However, earlier in Mark, Jesus had told his disciples exactly why he must die: "For even the Son of Man did not come to be served, but to serve, and to give His life—a ransom for many" (Mark 10:45). This is one of three related accounts in Mark where Jesus predicts his death (Mark 8:31–38; 9:30–35; 10:32–45). Even while facing the agony of what he was about to suffer, Jesus,

---

[12] For a recent treatment, see Andreas J. Köstenberger and Justin Taylor (with Alexander Stewart), *The Final Days of Jesus: The Most Important Week of the Most Important Person Who Ever Lived* (Wheaton: Crossway, 2014).

[13] See Andreas J. Köstenberger, L. Scott Kellum, and Charles L. Quarles, *The Cradle, the Cross, and the Crown: An Introduction to the New Testament* (Nashville: B&H Academic, 2009), 315.

according to Mark, stated in the garden of Gethsemane, "Get up; let's go! See—My betrayer is near" (Mark 14:42). This does not sound like a man who has lost control of the situation. Moreover, in the trial before the high priest, Jesus himself provides the testimony that led to the crucifixion (Mark 14:62). Therefore, while Luke does highlight Jesus' confidence in the face of suffering, this element is not absent in Mark. Furthermore, the deep anguish of Jesus, which Ehrman points out is prevalent in Mark, is evident in Luke as well. For instance, in Luke 22:42, Jesus asks the Father to remove the "cup" of his death. What is more, two verses later Luke describes Jesus as "being in anguish," with his sweat appearing "like drops of blood falling to the ground" (Luke 22:44). To be sure, Mark and Luke offer different perspectives on some of the particulars of Jesus' death as they write. Yet this does not mean their perspectives are in irreconcilable conflict.

Test Case 2: *The Gospels of Matthew and Luke mention Jesus' virgin birth while the Gospels of Mark and John are unaware of it.*

Matthew and Luke are the only two Gospels that explicitly affirm Jesus' virgin birth. But it is hardly the case that the other two canonical Gospels deny it or are unaware of it. Mark and John simply chose not to include the virgin birth in their accounts. As Ehrman well knows, any historical account is by nature selective, and the Gospels should not be regarded with skepticism simply because none of them includes every single detail that could have been mentioned. In fact, as John states explicitly at the end of his Gospel, this would have been a virtual impossibility (John 21:24–25). Like John (John 20:30–31) and all historians, ancient or modern, so all the Gospel writers were of necessity selective. Are there differences? Yes. Contradictions? Not so fast! The point of having four Gospels is having four different perspectives.[14]

---

[14] For a recent work challenging the historicity of the virgin birth, see Andreas T. Lincoln, *Born of a Virgin? Reconceiving Jesus in the Bible, Tradition, and Theology* (Grand Rapids: Eerdmans, 2013). But see the review by Andrews J. Köstenberger, accessed April 3, 2014, http://thegospelcoalition.org/book-reviews/review/born_of_a_virgin; and the more extensive review at http://www.biblicalfoundations.org/wp-content/uploads/2014/02/Born-of-a-Virgin.pdf.

In fact, it can plausibly be argued that both Mark and John were aware of the virgin birth, even though they don't make explicit reference to it. Mark, which many believe was the first Gospel written, is characteristically concise and, after a single opening verse, moves immediately into the ministry of John the Baptist (Mark 1:2–8) and then immediately into Jesus' baptism by John and Jesus' temptation in the wilderness (Mark 1:9–13) followed by Jesus' own ministry. Not only does Mark skip over the virgin birth, but he also skips over the entirety of Jesus' first thirty years of life. The reason for this is that Mark focuses his narrative on Jesus' ministry culminating in his crucifixion, so much so that one scholar, with an excusable touch of hyperbole, has dubbed Mark "a passion narrative with an extended introduction."[15]

It is an illegitimate argument from silence to contend that just because Mark does not mention it, he was unaware of the virgin birth. If taken to an extreme, this would mean Mark also did not know about a lot of other events he chose not to include. In the end one would have to argue that Mark knew nothing about Jesus' story except what he wrote about in his Gospel. This is not only illogical; it is patently absurd. It is also contrary to the universally accepted understanding, mentioned above, that all the biblical Gospels are by necessity selective. While it is therefore impossible to prove that Mark knew about the virgin birth, this is entirely possible and indeed likely from a historical standpoint because as a close associate of Peter and Paul and as a member of the early church (which was very close-knit) he would almost certainly have heard accounts of this remarkable supernatural event.

John, for his part, opens his Gospel with an even grander scene than the virgin birth, namely Jesus' preexistent glory with God the Father in the beginning. In this way John places the entirety of Jesus' subsequent ministry against the backdrop of his eternal preexistence with God the Father even prior to creation. Perhaps John may be forgiven for not including the virgin birth in

---

[15] Martin Kähler, *The So-Called Historical Jesus and the Historic Biblical Christ*, trans. Carl E. Braaten (Philadelphia: Fortress, 1964 [orig., *Der sogenannte historische Jesus und der geschichtliche, biblische Christus*, 1896]), 80n97. While nineteenth-century German theologian Martin Kähler was the first to describe it as such, since then so have a number of other scholars.

light of this even more sweeping affirmation of Jesus' eternal deity.
What is more, some have detected indirect references to the virgin
birth in John's Gospel, in particular in two passages. Later in John's
introduction to his Gospel, he speaks of those "who were born,
not of blood, or of the will of the flesh, or of the will of man, but
of God" (John 1:13), which to some suggests a hint of the virgin
birth in Jesus' case—especially since the next verse refers to the
fact that "the Word became flesh." Then, in the context of an acri-
monious interchange between Jesus and his Jewish opponents, the
latter sharply remark, "We weren't born of sexual immorality. . . .
We have one Father—God" (John 8:41). It is possible to hear here
the accusation that while the *Jews* weren't born of sexual immorality, *Jesus was*—which was the rumor that spread surrounding
the virgin birth (see Matt 1:18–25). In fact, later writings repeat
just this kind of charge, denying the paternity of God the Father
in Jesus' birth.[16]

Test Case 3: *In Matthew, Jesus refuses to perform a
miracle to prove his deity. By contrast, in
John, the spectacular deeds of Jesus are
not called "miracles" but "signs" to prove
and convince people of his true identity.*

A closer look at the Gospels reveals they contain both positive and negative remarks concerning Jesus' miracles. For instance,
while Jesus' signs are said to display his glory to his disciples in John
2:11, Jesus' initial reply to a call for help in John 4:48 denounces
people's dependence on "signs and wonders": "Unless you people
see signs and wonders, you will not believe." Moreover, in John,
Jesus implies that while any kind of faith is better than unbelief,
faith that must rely on miracles is inferior to faith on the basis
of reliable testimony. Jesus' response to the religious leaders' disbelief in John 10:37–38 serves as an example: "If I am not doing
My Father's works, don't believe Me. But if I am doing them and
you don't believe Me, *believe the works*" (emphasis added). Also, in

---

[16] See, e.g., *Gospel of Nicodemus* 2, which repeats the charge of Jesus' birth being the result of
fornication; and Origen, *Against Celsus* 1.28, according to which Jesus' birth was the result of
Mary's sexual union with Panthera, a Roman soldier.

his postresurrection conversation with Thomas, Jesus makes clear that it is more commendable for faith to be based on reliable testimony than on observing Jesus' signs (John 20:24–29). At the same time, while Jesus twice in Matthew (12:38–39; 16:1–4) refuses to perform a miracle on demand, he does indicate that miracles in some way function to elicit a positive response when denouncing cities "where most of His miracles were done, because they did not repent" (Matt 11:20).[17]

For Ehrman to try to pit John's testimony regarding miracles against the testimony of the other canonical Gospels, rather than reveal actual contradictions, illustrates his insensitivity to finer theological nuances in the theology of the New Testament. Ironically, he is missing the very thing he accuses conservatives of missing. In a recent essay I (Köstenberger) spent considerable time exploring the way John, writing subsequent to the three other biblical Gospels, theologically transposed various motifs found in Matthew, Mark, and Luke.[18] I identified close to twenty such instances, and the list could easily be augmented even further. In the case of John's theology of signs, he may have picked up on the only event identified as a "sign" in relation to Jesus in Matthew, Mark, and Luke: the "sign of Jonah," according to which Jonah was in the belly of the big fish for three nights and three days, which, according to Jesus, presaged the interval between Jesus' own death and resurrection. At the same time, those other Gospels regularly call Jesus' healings, nature miracles, and demon exorcisms "miracles" in order to highlight the powerful, even spectacular, nature of these acts.

John, as mentioned writing later, apparently sought to make the keen and decisive theological point that what was significant (or should we say "sign-ificant"?) was not the display of Jesus' power in and of itself; after all, what if people saw or even were the beneficiaries of one of Jesus' miracles but failed to perceive the

[17] D. A. Carson, "The Purpose of Signs and Wonders in the New Testament," in *Power Religion: The Selling Out of the Evangelical Church?*, ed. Michael Horton (Chicago: Moody, 1992), 89–118.

[18] Andreas J. Köstenberger, "John's Transposition Theology: Retelling the Story of Jesus in a Different Key," in *Earliest Christian History*, ed. Michael F. Bird and Jason Maston, Wissenschaftliche Untersuchungen zum Neuen Testament 2/320 (Tübingen: Mohr Siebeck, 2012), 191–226.

way in which the miracle pointed to who Jesus is (i.e., Messiah, Lord, and Savior)? In this case, John rightly perceived, Jesus' miracles did not serve their intended purpose, which clearly was not simply to wow people with a spectacular fireworks display of his power but to induce in them faith in the Messiah. Based on this rationale, John chose to designate the feats called "miracles" in Matthew, Mark, and Luke "signs," so as to make clear that what really mattered was the way Jesus' miracles served as signposts for people to recognize Jesus as the Messiah and Son of God. Someone who believes to identify a surface contradiction in the treatment of Jesus' miracles in the New Testament Gospels, therefore, merely nibbles at the edges, theologically speaking, rather than probing the demonstrable theological depth present in how John further develops the teaching of Matthew, Mark, and Luke.

Conversely, Luke notes how the miracles are signs without using the word. In Luke 11:20 Jesus says that if he casts out demons by the finger of God, then the kingdom of God has come upon Jesus' audience. This calls miracles signs without using the word. Acts says this outright using the word "signs" in Acts 2:22. The Gospels are not mutually contradictory as Ehrman claims.

Test Case 4: *Matthew and Paul are in contradiction on salvation and the law.*

In Pauline theology salvation could only come by believing in the death and resurrection of Jesus Christ apart from following the requirements of the Jewish law (see, e.g., Rom 3:21). The Law and the Prophets were meant to point to Jesus, God's ultimate solution. People must trust in Jesus Christ who has provided atonement for sin on the cross. Yet, according to Ehrman, Paul's theology on these points disagrees with Matthew's.

Working from Matthew 5:17–20, Ehrman explains that in Matthew the entire law is kept intact and must be kept. He writes,

> If Matthew, who wrote some twenty-five or thirty years after Paul, ever read any of Paul's letters, he certainly did not find them inspiring, let alone inspired. Matthew has a different view of the law

> from Paul. Matthew thinks that they as followers
> of Jesus need to keep the law. In fact, they need to
> keep it better even than most religious Jews, the
> scribes, and the Pharisees.[19]

For Ehrman, in Matthew to be "great" (Matt 5:19) meant keeping the least of the commandments, and getting into the kingdom meant keeping the law better than the Pharisees. On the other hand, for Paul "getting into the kingdom (a different way of saying being justified) is made possible only by the death and resurrection of Jesus; for gentiles, keeping the Jewish law (for example, circumcision) is strictly forbidden."[20]

Ehrman has brought up several issues that are fairly involved, and scholars have differed in how they understand the relationship between law and gospel.[21] This test case will therefore be a little more involved than the others, but this closer look is warranted by the significance of the matter and will prove helpful in unraveling the rather complicated theological issues involved. We will see not only how Ehrman has unsympathetically contrasted several emphases in Matthew and Paul but will also be struck by the shallowness of his assessment. In fact, contrary to Ehrman's claim, Matthew and Paul's theology have remarkable points of contact that testify to the unity of the writings included in the New Testament canon.

First, most Pauline scholars, while having various views on how works are to be understood in Paul's writings, have noted that in Paul as well it is important for Christians to keep the law. Though many understand this "law" to be some kind of New Testament ethic or the moral law of the Old Testament, nonetheless keeping the law is important. In the world of New Testament scholarship, there have been recent debates over what has been termed the "New Perspective" on Paul. One of the benefits of the debate has been the attention given to the significance of keeping the law in Paul's letters. For instance, one opponent of the New

---

[19] Ehrman, *Jesus, Interrupted*, 89.
[20] Ibid., 90.
[21] For a helpful overview of different views just in conservative scholarship, see Stanley Gundry, ed., *Five Views on Law and Gospel* (Grand Rapids: Zondervan, 1996).

Perspective believes this perspective emphasizes works incorrectly but has stressed nonetheless, "I believe it is *actually* true, not just hypothetically true, that God 'will render to each one according to his works: to those who by patience in well-doing seek for glory and honor and immortality, he will give eternal life' (Romans 2:6–7)."[22] The point here is not to moderate the debate on the New Perspective on Paul but to show simply there is wide consensus, even among those who disagree on significant points in Paul, that Paul views good works as a necessary part of the Christian life.

Second, careful reading of Matthew 5:17–20 in context shows that Jesus' teaching according to Matthew actually bears a remarkable resemblance to Paul's understanding of the law. In Matthew 5:17, "destroy" is set against "fulfill." In the context of Matthew, "fulfilled" should be understood within the story line of Scripture, with the Old Testament law pointing further to Jesus rather than simply as the opposite of "abolish," for this is how "fulfilled" is used throughout the rest of Matthew.[23] Understood in this way, Jesus claims that he in himself "fulfills" (i.e., "completes" or "brings to full expression") what the Law and the Prophets anticipated.

"Law" in Matthew 5:18 is not simply a reference to the precepts given in the Mosaic law or the moral law but rather refers to the Old Testament Scriptures in their entirety. Jesus is explaining in Matthew 5:18 that the Old Testament will remain authoritative and relevant until the end of the age as it is read in light of Jesus' fulfillment of it (Matt 5:17). In this vein Matthew 5:19 can be understood as a call to teach and submit to the law, but the law must be obeyed and taught not in its Old Testament manifestation but in and through Christ's fulfillment of the law. Jesus' point is that the ethical thrust of the law is kept by understanding what internal standard is being appealed to, and that is what is to be followed. So it is not murder but anger that matters, not divorce but lust, not an oath but the truth. Jesus calls for a fulfillment of the law by looking to the internal attitudes it is addressing. Matthew 5:20 links Jesus' announcement about his relation to the Old Testament

---

[22] John Piper, *The Future of Justification: A Response to N. T. Wright* (Wheaton: Crossway, 2007), 110.

[23] Matthew 1:22; 2:15, 17, 23; 4:14; 8:17; 12:17; 13:35; 21:4; 27:9.

and the specific teaching (Matt 5:17–19) that he is about to put forth (Matt 5:21–48). This reading of Matthew 5:17–20 is confirmed by what Jesus taught in Matthew 5:21–48 where Jesus is not simply extending or intensifying what Moses once said. In these subsequent verses Jesus is announcing that he has fulfilled the Old Testament and thus is elevating the Old Testament realities as the "lesser" gives way to the "greater." As Carson writes,

> By now it is clear that the Sermon on the Mount is not soporific sentimentality designed to induce a kind of feeble-minded do-goodism. Nor do these chapters tolerate the opinion that Jesus' view on righteousness has been so tempered with love that righteousness slips to a lower level than when its standard was dictated by the law. Instead, we discover that the righteousness demanded by Jesus surpasses anything imagined by the Pharisees, the strict orthodox religious group of Jesus' day. Christ's way is more challenging and more demanding—as well as more rewarding— than any legal system can ever be. Moreover, his way was prophetically indicated before it actually arrived, as Paul says, "But now a righteousness from God, apart from the law, has been made known, to which *the Law and the Prophets testify*" (Romans 3:21).[24]

Significantly, Carson references the connection between Romans 3:21 and the view of the law in the Sermon on the Mount, making explicit that he views those two passages as being in agreement rather than contradictory. What is more, these are by no means the only passages that link Matthew's and Paul's theology on Christians and the law. Another Pauline passage, Romans 10:4, affirms, "For Christ is *the end of the law* for righteousness to everyone who believes" (emphasis added). As usual in Paul's

---

[24] D. A. Carson, *Jesus' Sermon on the Mount: And His Confrontation with the World* (Grand Rapids: Baker, 1978), 41.

writings, "law" here likely refers to the Mosaic law. "End," which is the standard English translation for the original Greek word *telos*, is inherently and intentionally ambiguous. "End" could be referring to Christ being the "termination of the law" or to his serving as the "goal of the law." Most likely, the word in its present context combines both nuances and is best understood as conveying the sense of "culmination."[25] Paul is saying that the Mosaic law has reached its goal and therefore ceases to play the same central role it once had prior to Jesus' coming, though it is still relevant as it is seen through Christ.

Consequently, Matthew 5:17 and Romans 10:4 both portray Christ as the culmination of the Old Testament law. Jesus and Paul both caution against "undervaluing the degree to which Christ now embodies and mediates to us what the OT law was teaching and doing. Our relationship with God is now found in Christ, not through the law."[26] What is more, Douglas Moo has written concerning Romans 10:4 that "we find in Paul's teaching about Christ as the culmination of the law another evidence of the beautiful unity of the NT message. For what Paul says here is almost exactly what Jesus claims in one of his most famous theological pronouncements [Matt 5:17]."[27] Romans 3:21 and 10:4 are but two examples of passages from Paul that are similar to this understanding of Matthew.

Third, in Matthew there are also indications that while works are important, individuals are not meant to count on the law to make them right with God. It appears that "Paul explains the function of the law; and what Paul is explaining in Romans and Galatians, Jesus is doing in the Sermon on the Mount [and throughout the Gospel of Matthew]."[28] In Jesus' famous sermon in

---

[25] Douglas J. Moo, "The Law of Christ as the Fulfillment of the Law of Moses," in *Five Views on Law and Gospel*, ed. Stanley N. Gundry (Grand Rapids: Zondervan, 1996), 358.

[26] Douglas J. Moo, *The Epistle to the Romans*, New International Commentary on the New Testament (Grand Rapids: Eerdmans, 1996), 642–43.

[27] Ibid., 642.

[28] Carson, *Sermon on the Mount*, 128. For an example of a responsible treatment on the relationship between Paul and Jesus, see David Wenham, *Paul: Founder of Christianity or Follower of Jesus?* (Grand Rapids: Eerdmans, 1996). See also the review by Andreas Köstenberger in *Trinity Journal* 16 (1995): 259–62, accessed April 3, 2014, http://www.biblicalfoundations.org/wp-content/uploads/2012/01/06-TrinJ-Paul-Follower-of-Jesus-or-Founder.pdf.

Matthew, he begins with a call for poverty of spirit and urges people to admit their desperate spiritual condition before God. Jesus'
call to live out kingdom priorities has the effect of both making
disciples and of making people conscious of their inadequacies.
Not only does Jesus' Sermon on the Mount leave people feeling
convicted of falling short of such high standards (Matt 5:27–48),
but it also ends with a call to pray to God for his favor, which is
essential for entrance into the kingdom (Matt 7:7–11). For this
reason people should petition the Father (Matt 7:7–11) and ask
him to forgive their sin (Matt 6:12).

Nevertheless, Jesus and Paul clearly do have different (though
not incompatible) ways of addressing the matter of salvation. And
the danger of reading Paul into Matthew (or any of the Gospels)
is always there, especially for those who see an inherent unity in
the New Testament. The danger on the other end of the spectrum,
however, is to see the development from Jesus' to Paul's teaching as
a sign of conflicting theologies. Instead, there is an understandable
progression from Jesus to Paul. Jesus is preaching to people before
they have witnessed his death and resurrection. His listeners have
yet to grapple with the theological implications of the event, which
each of the Gospels is careful to narrate. After all, Jesus' own disciples, even after they were told repeatedly, did not accept that Jesus
was actually going to die and then rise again.

Consequently, to flesh out the theological implications that
would flow from the event (as Paul does) would have been prema-
ture and is something Jesus left for his disciples to do subsequent
to his death. The fact that the Gospel writers did not put a full
theological explanation of Jesus' death, burial, and resurrection on
the lips of Jesus in the Gospels is a testimony to their commitment
to truthfulness and historical veracity. The Gospels each highlight
Jesus' death and resurrection by narrating these events in considerable detail and by making them the climax of their stories. Even
though they wrote after Paul's letters, the evangelists did not alter
the words of Jesus to make him sound exactly like Paul. Yet once
the Gospels and Paul's writings are understood at their respective
junctures in salvation history, the unity of the New Testament

amid their legitimate diversity becomes apparent, and diversity is rightly seen as a virtue rather than a liability.

The test cases surveyed above demonstrate that Ehrman's own biases have resulted in rushed judgments and superficial interpretation. Rather than maintaining the stance of a fair-minded observer who recognizes that all stories are told from particular perspectives, Ehrman has mistakenly equated good scholarship with skeptical scholarship. This has led one recent reviewer to respond,

> Unfortunately, Ehrman's discussion proves to be remarkably shallow and exhibits no awareness of the major issues or categories. . . . In the end, his theological objections are similar to the kind one might read on an internet blog or web chat room; they may have a lot of zeal behind them, but stem from only a cursory reading of the biblical text and exhibit little real understanding of the issues.[29]

Claim 2:   *Attempts to reconcile various events in the New Testament are mistaken because such harmonizations create another account that is different from the ones being read.*

Ehrman's stance against harmonizations is curious considering the limitations of the discipline of ancient historiography. Due to the lack of source documents and a particular writer's inability to say everything about an event from all possible perspectives, ancient historians, no matter the topic of research, regularly harmonized various accounts to get a complete picture of the particular event being studied. Historians understand that their job is to put together "what actually happened" from the various resources available to them, but Ehrman says it is illegitimate to reconstruct from the Gospels a unified account of what happened. Thus right from the start, by refusing to acknowledge the legitimacy of the

---

[29] Kruger, "Review of *Jesus, Interrupted.*"

ordinary practice of historians, Ehrman seeks to validate his conclusion: the New Testament, in particular the Gospels, cannot
be harmonized.

Harmonization can be a somewhat messy process in spots.
We admit that. Like in a courtroom, a few loose ends can pop up
where the pieces don't exactly fit together. But in case after case
in Scripture—as seen in the test cases we studied earlier in the
chapter—solid arguments can be made for why they appear the
way they do.

Let us provide an example, which doesn't relate solely to the harmonization question but does speak to how a rational argument can
counter what many skeptics consider a slam-dunk contradiction.

Matthew 12:1–8; Mark 2:23–28; and Luke 6:1–5 include a
story where Jesus and his disciples were walking through a grain
field on the Sabbath day, picking off heads of grain as they went.
When spotted by some Pharisees, Jesus and his men found themselves accused of breaking the law.

Jesus responded to the charge by recalling a thousand-year-old
scene from King David's early life (1 Sam 21:1–6) when David and
his young band of warriors stopped off hungry at the high priest's
door but found the only bread in the house was the sacred loaves
dedicated for the worship of God. Yet the priest decided to give
them the consecrated bread anyway. This priest's name, according
to 1 Samuel 21, was Ahimelech.

Mark is the only one of the Gospel writers who, when recounting this event, chose to identify the Old Testament story to which
Jesus had referred (Mark 2:26) by saying it occurred when there
was a high priest named Abiathar.

So which is it? Ahimelech or Abiathar?

This was the touchstone that sent Bart Ehrman over the edge
of confidence in the Bible. If the God who supposedly created and
maintains the atmospheric chemistry of planet Earth cannot keep
one of his Gospel writers from going to the "High Priests Starting
with Letter A" stack and picking the wrong card, how can he still
expect us to believe he is so all wise and powerful?

It's certainly possible that these two names got confused, if not
originally, then at some point along the way. Anybody can see that.

But there are also reasonable explanations.

For instance, the Greek word *epi* used in Mark 2:26 right before "Abiathar the high priest" is normally translated "upon." But in this case that would make little sense. Two other prime candidates for the meaning of *epi* could help us make sense of what Mark was saying. First, it is possible that Mark used *epi* to indicate the time the event occurred.

When people talk about the climate of American culture that existed during the Eisenhower administration—the relatively easy, prosperous days of innocence and optimism following World War II, they're basically meaning the decade of the 1950s. Well, Eisenhower wasn't inaugurated until January 1953. So when people refer to the national mood under Eisenhower, are they referring only to the eight specific years of his presidency? Or do they mean a general block of time including and on either end of those years?

Abiathar, who was the much more recognizable high-priestly name from that era in history, having been the sole survivor of King Saul's maniacal slaughter of priests in 1 Samuel 22, would have been the quickest connection point for Mark's first-century audience.

Something similar appears to be going on in Luke 3:2 where Annas and Caiaphas are both said to be high priests during Jesus' ministry, even though both men were not officially the high priest at the same time. But no one accuses Luke of making an error here. Why? Because it is accepted that while Caiaphas was actually the official high priest, his father-in-law Annas was a significant figure who could still be called the high priest. Why couldn't Mark be doing something similar in referring to the time of Abiathar, who would come to be known as the high priest? He very well could have been.

Second, if *epi* is not referring to time here, it could be indicating location. Today, if you want to refer to an Old Testament passage, it's as easy as citing the chapter and verse numbers. But in Mark's day there were no chapter and verse numbers. Chapter and verse numbers were added much later. So if a writer wanted to point to a location in Scripture without quoting the entire passage, he might simply mention a significant figure or object in the Old Testament passage. In fact, later in his Gospel, Mark does this using the word *epi* within a phrase that is translated "the passage about [or, entitled] the burning bush" (Mark 12:26). Since the passage from 1 Samuel that Mark 2:26 is referencing falls right before the first scenes involving Abiathar, and he was the more notable of the two priests, it would not be unusual for Mark to use Abiathar as a sort of title for the section of Scripture to which he is referring. While these two arguments may not solve every question surrounding Abiathar's appearance in Mark 2, they are at least reasonable hypotheses. We wish Ehrman was still open to considering some of these other rationales because, as with every other contradiction the Bible is accused of, it's just not as open-and-shut as the skeptics suggest.

To give just one more example, according to Ehrman the accounts of Jesus' trial before Pontius Pilate as recorded in Mark and John are contradictory because Mark's account is "short and straightforward," with Jesus not saying much and Pilate not declaring Jesus innocent, while John's account is longer, Jesus having a lot more to say, and Pilate declaring Jesus to be innocent.[30] We can agree that there are some differences here, but why Ehrman insists the differences must be discrepancies is difficult to understand. What we have, instead, is differing perspectives by different authors on the same event. John includes details absent from Mark, but only unwarranted skepticism forces these two perspectives into contradiction.[31] The same phenomenon can also be observed in classical literature.

These kinds of harmonies are an accepted practice of secular historians. As Gilbert Garraghan has stated, "[A]lmost any critical history that discusses the evidence for important statements will furnish examples of discrepant or contradictory accounts and the attempts which are made to reconcile them."[32] Craig Blomberg has demonstrated how the different approaches to harmonizing the New Testament are appropriately applied to other works to

---

[30] Ehrman, *Jesus, Interrupted*, 43–45.

[31] Again, see Köstenberger, "John's Transposition Theology," which makes a plausible case that John may have been familiar with Mark's Gospel and chose to supplement it rather than merely repeat what Mark already said.

[32] G. J. Garraghan, *A Guide to the Historical Method* (New York: Fordham, 1946), 314; cited in Craig L. Blomberg, "The Legitimacy and Limits of Harmonization," in *Hermeneutics, Authority, and Canon*, ed. D. A. Carson and John D. Woodbridge (Grand Rapids: Zondervan, 1986), 144.

better understand history when multiple sources attest to the same events.[33] Blomberg provides numerous examples of legitimate harmonization from Josephus's *Antiquities* and *War* and from Arrian's life of Alexander and Plutarch's biography of Alexander. Blomberg concludes his investigation by noting that the more one studies how historical conclusions are drawn from extrabiblical sources, "the more inescapable the legitimacy of harmonization becomes."[34]

N. T. Wright puts it a little more pointedly: "I am, after all, suggesting no more than that Jesus be studied like any other figure of the ancient past. Nobody grumbles at a book on Alexander the Great if, in telling the story, the author 'harmonizes' two or three sources; that is his or her job, to advance hypotheses which draw together the data into a coherent framework rather than leaving it scattered. Of course, sources on Alexander, like sources on Jesus, Tiberius, Beethoven, Gandhi or anybody else, have their own point of view, which must be taken carefully into account."[35] In light of Ehrman's resistance to harmonizing the biblical material, it wouldn't be surprising if Ehrman "grumbled" when any kind of harmony is accepted in these various writings, but this would say more about Ehrman's own skeptical presuppositions than about the legitimacy of the common approach of harmonizing historical accounts.

Claim 3:   *The Gospels' chronological differences*
                are historical contradictions.

Ehrman's critique stands only if someone were to try to make the Gospels into something they were never intended to be. Ancient literature from this time period often did not narrate events in the exact chronological order. Instead, historical events were arranged for thematic and topical reasons. This is clearly seen in the Gospels as each author felt the freedom to arrange parables, sayings, and other events in view of their particular purposes. The first readers of the Gospels would have expected these kinds of topical arrangements. Only the most fundamentalist interpreter would expect the

---

[33] Blomberg, "Legitimacy and Limits of Harmonization," 135–74.
[34] Ibid., 173.
[35] N. T. Wright, *Jesus and the Victory of God* (Minneapolis: Fortress, 1996), 88.

Gospels to fit rigid modern standards of chronology. Ironically, Ehrman demonstrates that his own fundamentalist presuppositions die hard.

For example, Ehrman cries foul when Luke's Gospel places the tearing of the veil in the temple before Jesus' death while Mark puts it after the crucifixion. Nevertheless, there appears to be a simple reason for this rearrangement. Luke likely mentions the tearing of the veil prior to the crucifixion in order to put it beside other cosmic signs he gives. In other words, Luke is providing a list of cosmic signs without claiming any particular order for these events. This type of flexibility in chronology, as mentioned, is frequent not only in the Gospels but in other ancient literature. Once fundamentalist presuppositions are shed and the Gospels are allowed to be what they were intended to be, Ehrman's claims of chronological contradictions appear more skeptical than scholarly.

Claim 4:   *The Gospels are so different in detail that they must be deemed in error at numerous points and cannot be viewed as divinely inspired.*

No serious scholar denies that the Gospels at times differ in details. But once again, differences do not necessarily mean contradictions. For one, Ehrman inadequately appreciates the nature of Jesus' teaching ministry. Jesus would travel from town to town, teaching several of the same lessons and parables in slightly different ways. If he taught a lesson once, he no doubt would have taught the same lesson on several other occasions. This not only helped carve the sayings and lessons in the minds of the disciples; it also meant there was some variation in how Jesus told particular stories or taught certain truths. As we speak at different places, we are often asked to address topics we have written or spoken about previously. Consequently, we often find ourselves saying similar things in different ways. No doubt Jesus did the same, and this accounts for some of the variations in the Gospels.

Jesus also likely taught different moral lessons using similar wording. For example, Ehrman implies that Matthew 12:30 and Mark 9:40 are contradictory because in Matthew Jesus says, "Anyone who is not with Me is against Me," while in Mark Jesus says, "Whoever is not against us is for us." Ehrman suggests that one of the evangelists simply got confused. However, Luke apparently believed Jesus made *both* of these remarks at different times and did not view them as contradictory since he included both in his Gospel (Luke 9:50; 11:23). What is more, the contexts of Matthew 12:30 and Mark 9:40 are different. In Matthew, Jesus is aiming his comments at those who attributed Jesus' ministry to evil forces; in Mark, Jesus is acknowledging the legitimacy of someone who is casting out demons in Jesus' name. In light of the respective contexts, the most natural explanation is that Jesus uttered the two statements at different times. While the message conveyed by these two sayings is not identical, neither is it contradictory.

Ehrman also unfairly forces modern expectations for history writing onto first-century history. When the New Testament was written, there were no printers, newspapers, CDs, mp3s, jump drives, blogs, or recording devices. The first century was an oral culture where writers were free to report history by the use of paraphrasing, summarizing, and even explaining someone's words, not merely quoting them. In view of the accepted practices of their culture, it is best to understand the Gospels as containing Jesus' "very voice" rather than his "very words," though there are certainly places where we have Jesus' actual words (especially in Aramaic expressions such as *Talitha koum!* ["Little girl, . . . get up!" Mark 5:41] or *Eloi, Eloi, lemá sabachtháni?* ["My God, My God, why have You forsaken Me?" Mark 15:34]). Several factors have made this the accepted position in conservative scholarship for quite some time.[36]

First, Jesus probably taught mostly in Aramaic while the Gospels were written in Greek. Therefore, most of Jesus' teachings in the Gospels are actually translations of Jesus' original teaching in Aramaic into Greek, and translations may invariably differ.

Second, most of the accounts of Jesus in the Gospels include him saying only a few sentences at a time. However, the Gospels tell us that he taught for hours at a time (e.g., Mark 6:34–36). In light of this, it seems likely that the authors of the Gospels recorded

---

[36] See Darrell L. Bock, "The Words of Jesus in the Gospels: Live, Jive, or Memorex?," in *Jesus Under Fire*, ed. Michael J. Wilkins and J. P. Moreland (Grand Rapids: Zondervan, 1995), 73–99.

shorter summaries of the actual sermons or speeches, which were considerably longer when they were originally given.

Third, the New Testament writers, when quoting a given passage from the Old Testament, often don't cite the source text word for word (though at other times they do). Instead, they exhibit a certain amount of freedom in adapting the source text to their own context or in stressing a particular aspect they want to bring out. For this reason it should not be surprising to see the Gospel writers doing the same thing in recording the words of Jesus.

With this kind of flexibility allowed in wording, Ehrman's arguments that insist the Gospels are contradictory because of variations in wording are unfounded. For example, he argues that the centurion present at Jesus' crucifixion calls Jesus "God's Son" in Mark (15:39) while, in contradiction to this, he calls him "righteous" in Luke (23:47). But, as has been noted,

> He doesn't consider the fact that one's righteous status is surely implied in the title 'son of God,' making these terms fairly interchangeable depending on the emphasis desired by the author. Given Mark's preference for the 'son of God' theme (1:1), and given Luke's concern to prove to the authorities that Jesus (and Christians) were innocent (1:3–4), these differences are quite intelligible.[37]

That we are given the "very voice" of Jesus in the Gospels is hardly surprising once one considers the historical nature of the Christian faith. Jesus lived in a historical culture (first-century Judaism), and his teachings were heard and recorded in the context of that culture. Ehrman has once again set the Gospels up for failure by assuming with very narrow and rigid expectations what the Gospels should look like and then criticizing them for not meeting his unreasonable and anachronistic standards.

---

[37] Kruger, "Review of *Jesus, Interrupted.*"

Claim 5:   *The diversity of views within the New*
            Testament indicates that "Jesus was not
            originally considered to be God in any
            sense at all. . . . he eventually became divine
            for his followers in some sense before
            he came to be thought of as equal with
            God Almighty in an absolute sense."[38]

Bart Ehrman has experienced somewhat of an evolution himself on the subject of Christology. In critiquing the then wildly
popular *The Da Vinci Code* in 2004, Ehrman recognized that in
Philippians and other early Christian writings, including multiple Gospels, Jesus is presented as "equal with God" and "divine."[39]
In *Jesus, Interrupted* (2009), in a very different line of reasoning,
he claims, "John is our only Gospel that actually speaks of Jesus
as divine" and argues that this belief was particular to the late
first-century community from which John's Gospel originated.[40]
However, another shift occurred in Ehrman's most recent book,
How Jesus Became God, in which he now recognizes that belief in
Jesus' divinity was remarkably early—the catch is that he believes
this early view meant something far less significant than what most
Christians now mean when referring to "Jesus' divinity." Ehrman
argues for a trajectory in early Christian thought that evolved from
Jesus being "not . . . God in any sense at all" to him being "divine . . .
in some sense" to him being "equal with God Almighty in an absolute sense."[41] This certainly has the advantage of being fairly tidy:
the early Christian understanding of Jesus' identity simply evolved

---

[38] Bart D. Ehrman, *How Jesus Became God: The Exaltation of a Jewish Preacher from Galilee*
(San Francisco: HarperCollins, 2014), 44.

[39] Bart D. Ehrman, *Truth and Fiction in The Da Vinci Code: A Historian Reveals What We
Really Know about Jesus, Mary Magdalene, and Constantine* (New York: Oxford University
Press, 2004), 16: "For Paul—and presumably for the Philippians to whom he wrote—Christ was
'in the form' of God and was, in some sense, equal with God, even though he became human.
Similar teachings can be found in other writings of the New Testament. One of Jesus' common
designations throughout these writings is 'Son of God.' This is scarcely an epithet that came to be
applied to Jesus on the basis of a close vote at the Council of Nicaea hundreds of years later. Our
earliest Gospel, that of Mark, begins by announcing its subject matter: 'The beginning of the
Gospel of Jesus Christ, the son of God' (Mark 1:1)." Ehrman also appears to indicate that Jesus'
divinity is not limited to one Gospel only: "The Gospels of the New Testament portray him as
human as much as they portray him as divine" (15).

[40] Ehrman, *Jesus, Interrupted*, 248–52.

[41] Ehrman, *How Jesus Became God*, 44.

from a low to a very high view. Yet, while Ehrman's provocative proposal might play well to those who are hungry for a conspiracy theory, a closer look reveals problems with his reading of the evidence. We'll start with two preliminary issues concerning how Ehrman makes his argument in *How Jesus Became God* and then get into some of the major planks of his proposal.[42]

First, Ehrman makes his case by painting a rather monolithic portrait of scholarship on the issue. With his all-too-common rhetoric, he implies that there are sober-minded, realistic historians, that is, "the majority of critical scholars," who "for more than a century" have maintained that Jesus was an apocalyptic prophet and concur that Jesus didn't even claim to be divine.[43] The problem is that Ehrman once again has not really given his readers the whole story. In fact, on the same day *How Jesus Became God* was released, a five-scholar team (Michael F. Bird, Craig A. Evans, Simon J. Gathercole, Charles E. Hill, and Chris Tilling) published a full-fledged response to Ehrman called *How God Became Jesus: The Real Origins of Belief in Jesus' Divine Nature.*[44] Bird and company take up most of the major individual pieces of Ehrman's argument and subject them to critical scrutiny. We'll summarize and build on some of what they said below. But it's important to take note of what's going on here: Ehrman should not claim to speak for the majority of serious scholars when this volume includes five "first-rate scholars" who teach on three continents and in four countries (Australia, Canada, England, the United States) at institutions such as Cambridge University.[45]

Paradigms are frequently proposed in scholarship, and Ehrman certainly has every right to try his hand at a model for understanding early Christology. However, when proposals

---

[42] For a general critique and assessment, see Andreas Köstenberger's review of Ehrman's *How Jesus Became God* at http://thegospelcoalition.org/book-reviews/review/how_jesus_became_god.

[43] Ehrman, *How Jesus Became God*, 6.

[44] Michael F. Bird, Craig A. Evans, Simon J. Gathercole, Charles E. Hill, and Chris Tilling, *How God Became Jesus: The Real Origins of Belief in Jesus' Divine Nature: A Response to Bart D. Ehrman* (Grand Rapids: Zondervan, 2014). See Andreas J. Köstenberger's review at http://thegospelcoalition.org/book-reviews/review/how_god_became_jesus.

[45] In a news article about the two books (http://www.huffingtonpost.com/2014/03/25/bart-ehrman-jesus-god_n_5029457.html), Ehrman reportedly "lauds his five sparring partners as first-rate scholars."

are offered, the expectation is that the author will engage with
the best of those who went before him.[46] However, in this case,
Ehrman rarely engages with the best of "high Christology" scholarship. Two of the most distinguished scholars on the subject of
Christology in the early church are Richard Bauckham (University
of St Andrews) and Larry Hurtado (University of Edinburgh).[47] In
How Jesus Became God Ehrman never even mentions the work of
Richard Bauckham, who has done some of the most penetrating
and careful research on early Christology. Bauckham's work is a
prominent force to be reckoned with if one is going to throw his
own Christological proposal on the table, yet Ehrman does not
engage with him at all. Not even a footnote! And while he does
mention Larry Hurtado twice, he not only fails to offer any substantial responses, but takes him out of context and uses him in
support of a position Hurtado actually denies holding![48]

Second, Ehrman's approach to the process of historical
inquiry predetermines that he will reach skeptical conclusions
about the person of Jesus. Through the years scholars have created certain criteria for validating the various events and sayings
in the life of Jesus. For instance, one of these criteria of authenticity
is called "multiple attestation." According to this criterion, a saying or event can be validated historically if the saying or event is
attested in multiple traditions. However, many scholars from vary-
ing theological perspectives have rightly tempered expectations

---

[46] The expectation is that this type of engagement will at least occur in an academic work that
can stand behind more popular versions.

[47] Richard Bauckham, *God Crucified: Monotheism and Christology in the New Testament*
(Carlisle, UK: Paternoster, 1988); repr. as *Jesus and the God of Israel: God Crucified and Other
Studies on the New Testament's Christology of Divine Identity* (Milton Keynes, UK: Paternoster,
2008); Larry Hurtado, *One God, One Lord: Early Christian Devotion and Ancient Monotheism*,
2nd ed. (London: T&T Clark, 1998); idem, *Lord Jesus Christ: Devotion to Jesus in Earliest Christianity* (Grand Rapids: Eerdmans, 2003).

[48] Ehrman (*How Jesus Became God*, 61) cites Hurtado's work to support the claim that early
Christians used principal angel speculation in prior Jewish thought to justify putting Jesus next
to God. Yet, Hurtado is not saying that the early Christians thought of Jesus as an angel; he is
simply making a comparison. On this point, Michael F. Bird, in *How God Became Jesus*, cites
Hurtado making his larger point, which apparently Ehrman misses: "I have demonstrated in
One God, One Lord, we have no analogous accommodation of a second figure along with God as
recipient of such devotion in the Jewish tradition of the time, making it very difficult to fit this
inclusion of Christ as recipient of devotion into any known devotional pattern attested among
Jewish groups of the Roman period" ("Of Gods, Angels, and Men," in *How God Became Jesus*,
38–39; cf. Hurtado, *Lord Jesus Christ*, 50).

for what these criteria can demonstrate. After all, picking apart a 2,000-year-old document to try to map out what Gospel tradition comes from where is a bit like predicting who will win the World Series next year. There are some basic conclusions you can reasonably draw (it probably won't be the Cubs), but even the "experts" are going to have some very different opinions. In any case, the most these various criteria can do is bolster an event's historical likelihood; they cannot deny the event or saying. To use the example of multiple attestation, even if an event is only in one source, this does not prove the event didn't happen. In the eyes of a fair historian, failing to meet a criterion simply means that there is no more evidence available to confirm, not that there is sufficient reason to deny. Does only one witness at the scene of a crash invalidate that witness's testimony? Of course not. Would four collaborating witnesses bolster the evidence for the testimony given? Absolutely! But just because there is only one eyewitness in the first scenario doesn't mean that the testimony of the one witness is false or lacks credibility.

Nevertheless, even at times when the criterion of multiple attestation is met, seemingly bolstering the evidence for the saying or event's historicity, Ehrman simply ignores the criterion. For instance, Ehrman believes that Jesus only used the expression "Son of Man" to refer to another figure, not himself, who would later come. The problem for Ehrman is that the "Son of Man" sayings by Jesus in reference to himself meet the "multiple attestation" criterion. In addition, it was an exceptional usage; it was not the church's favorite title for Jesus.[49] Yet Ehrman never notes any of this. As objective as he claims to be, the fact is his readers only get half (or less) of the scholarly story.

Interestingly enough, it appears that by using certain criteria to deem events and sayings nonhistorical, Ehrman is claiming a type of absolute certainty for historical inquiry that he accuses Christian apologists of possessing. We think Ehrman is right to claim there is a problem when Christian apologists suggest they can prove with certainty that Jesus was God and rose from the

---

[49] Bird, "Did Jesus Think He Was God?," in *How God Became Jesus*, 61–67.

grave. We are certainly not making this claim ourselves. Instead, we are saying that the evidence, if one is open to it, points one to a remarkable early paradigm shift in these Jewish monotheists, a shift that is best explained by Jesus' unique claims concerning himself and his post-resurrection appearances. Though ironically, by using criteria to deny certain testimony about Jesus, Ehrman is himself suggesting that *he can know*—with what seems to be a kind of confidence he once had as an apologist—what *Jesus did not say and do*. Ehrman admits that he once was a Christian apologist who used many of the arguments he now, as a historian, must refute. However, in actuality, it seems now he has only switched sides. In all these years he still has his fundamentalist mentality in evaluating truth claims. Now he is an *unbelieving apologist*. He no longer believes the resurrection can be proven, but now instead believes he can demonstrate the alternatives. Yet Ehrman's conclusions are rooted in an even deeper problem, a problem that actually closes him off to considering possible historical explanations.

In a revealing section of *How Jesus Became God*, Ehrman explains his approach to history. He writes, "It is not appropriate for a historian to presuppose a perspective or worldview that is not generally held."[50] "Held by whom?" we ask. Later he writes, "History, as established by historians, is based only on shared presuppositions."[51] We should first point out that since the beginning of the discipline most historians have been doing "history" (at least that is what they thought they were doing) without naturalistic assumptions. In the above quotes, Ehrman surely has in mind those whom he and others (who share his assumptions) have allowed to be their discussion partners. Is there a first-world, Western post-Enlightenment bias at work, not shared by many in the rest of our current world? There are plenty of historians who do not share his naturalistic presuppositions. Some temporarily adopt these naturalistic presuppositions for a place at the table with Ehrman's brand of history (which can be a helpful exercise), and others are not willing to let those with naturalistic presuppositions always set the terms of engagement. Why should they? Because, so

---

[50] Ehrman, *How Jesus Became God*, 146.
[51] Ibid., 150.

we are told by the "real historians," "real historians" don't presuppose that God can intervene in the world. But why don't the "real historians" allow for the possibility? And, please remind us, who decides who the "real historians" are in the first place?[52] Don't miss the circular reasoning here.

In short, for Ehrman historical inquiry cannot allow for any possibility, and certainly not point to any conclusion, that God is involved in the world in specific ways. Hence, historic Christian conclusions are off the table before anyone ever sits down, even though Ehrman's justification for such a move is far from convincing.[53] We will return to this point as we wrap up this response, but now that you have seen some of the problems with Ehrman's general approach in *How Jesus Became God*, we want to direct attention to some issues with the major planks of his argument.

First, in contrast to Ehrman's claim, Christianity did not elevate Jesus to a demi-god (little "g") as a result of interface with pagan and Jewish traditions and as an initial step toward being recognized later as God (big "G"). Ehrman spends quite a bit of space giving evidence of what he describes as the "pyramid" understanding of deities in the culture at large, with people believing in various lesser gods and one supreme god. While there is always a

---

[52] In any case, if, according to Ehrman, "it is not appropriate for a historian to presuppose a perspective or worldview that is not generally held," one wonders what he would do if he moved to teach and do research in one of the many places in the world where the overwhelming majority of historians do not share his anti-supernatural presuppositions? Or if the tide changed in his particular peer group? Would he claim that they all aren't "real historians" even though he is in the minority? Or would he claim they all need to adopt a different set of better presuppositions?

[53] Ehrman chides any historian who would "presuppose her conclusions and try to locate only the evidence that supports those presupposed conclusions" (*How Jesus Became God*, 146). However, this is exactly what Ehrman admittedly does. He claims the historian cannot conclude that a supernatural event caused the empty tomb but instead can "come up with perfectly sensible other solutions as to why a once occupied tomb may have become empty: someone stole the body; someone innocently decided to move the body to another tomb; the whole story was in fact a legend, that is, the burial and discovery of an empty tomb were tales the later Christians invented to persuade others that the resurrection indeed happened" (149). Or "the historian can look into the question of whether the disciples really had visions of Jesus after his death. People have visions all the time." But, "What historians cannot conclude, however, as historians, is that the disciples had visions of Jesus after he was really, actually dead and that it was because Jesus really, actually appeared to them alive after God had raised him from the dead. This conclusion would be rooted in theological presuppositions not generally held by all historians" (149). In following Ehrman's words on page 146, he presupposes his conclusion (which is that whatever happened, God does not intervene in the world) and then will only consider evidence that supports his presupposed conclusion (i.e., God does not intervene in the world).

danger of "parallelomania"[54]—a fallacy with which Ehrman seems to be flirting—background material is important because early Christians were clearly aware of the culture around them (see, e.g., 1 Cor 8:4–6; 10:20–21; Acts 14:12–13; Col 2:18; Jude 9, 14). It seems that the New Testament authors at times, much like modern missionaries in a foreign culture, were seeking to make connections with the culture around them, using language and categories people could understand and at the same time often redefining such categories. One of Ehrman's mistakes here is skipping too quickly over the uniqueness of the Christian claims concerning Jesus in comparison with all possible parallels. As Michael Bird puts it (with what is becoming classic "Bird humor"):

> For instance, the worship of a crucified and risen Messiah was definitely unique and incredibly scandalous to all audiences, whether Jewish or Greek. To Jewish audiences, worshiping a crucified man was blasphemy; it was about as kosher as pork sausages wrapped in bacon served to Jews for a jihad fundraiser. To Greeks, worshipping a man recently raised from the dead was like doing obeisance to the first zombie you met in a zombie apocalypse. If Christian ideas about God were so snug and down within the ancient world, then why was Paul flogged by the Jewish communities (2 Cor 11:24) and laughed out of the Athenian Areopagus by Greek philosophers (Acts 17:32)? Could it be that the Christian idea of God was startling, odd, and even offensive to Jews and pagans, who had trouble swallowing its claims about Jesus?[55]

---

[54] "Parallelomania" is an exegetical fallacy in which a litany of cultural parallels (possibly from various cultures) are drawn upon with the assumption that because there are some analogous aspects, these connections must have been intentional and/or are determinative for meaning.

[55] Bird, "Of Gods, Angels, and Men," in *How God Became Jesus,* 26–27.

In line with this quotation from Bird, the contributions of Hurtado and Bauckham are important. The early Christian view of Jesus has appropriately been labeled a revised form of monotheism or what is sometimes referred to as "Christological monotheism." While there were undoubtedly exceptions here and there, devout first-century Jews—such as the very first disciples—were strict monotheists who only worshipped one God, the Creator of all things (e.g., Deut 6:4; Isa 45:5–7; 1 Macc 1:24–25; Rom 1:25; 11:36; 1 Cor 8:4–6).[56] These were not pagans who worshipped many gods, nor were they Jews who had radically departed from what most Jewish children grew up hearing and repeating time and again: "The LORD our God, the LORD is One" (Deut 6:4). And yet, they worshipped Jesus! And this worship began immediately rather than growing incrementally. Hurtado makes this point well when he writes, "This concern to define and reverence Jesus with reference to the one God is what I mean by the term 'binitarian.' Here we see the powerful effect of Jewish monotheism, combined with a strong impetus to reverence Jesus in *unprecedented* ways, in the innovative and vigorous devotional pattern advocated and reflected in Paul's letters."[57]

Second Temple intermediary figures fall short as precedents to the exaltation of Jesus to divine status because, as created beings, these were acknowledged to be distinct from God or to represent personifications of God (e.g., Wisdom). In other words, Ehrman is sloppy in the way he defines the terms "divine" and "angels," and this imprecision gives him a rhetorical advantage with his general audience.[58] There is a big difference between transcendence and

---

[56] Simon Gathercole, "What Did the First Christians Think about Jesus?," in *How God Became Jesus*, makes an important point: "Matthew, Mark, and Luke, however, imply that the Jewish milieu, which Jesus inhabited, was one in which there was a strict God/creation divide. The scribes in Mark 2, for example, do not think that Jesus' forgiveness of sins was an interesting experiment in the degree to which a human being might participate in the divine realm, but accused Jesus of blasphemy, as one crossing the creator/creature boundary and encroaching upon divine privileges; the same is true, as we have seen, in Mark 14" (101). He goes on to cite the views of Paul—not only Paul the apostle but Paul the former Pharisee—as evidence for the milieu in which Jesus and his followers lived. A fixture in Paul's theology is the absolute barrier between the Creator God and the created (e.g., Rom 1:25; 11:36).

[57] Hurtado, *Lord Jesus Christ*, 151–52; cf. Bird, "Of Gods, Angels, and Men," 30.

[58] For more on this, see Chris Tilling, "Problems with Ehrman's Interpretative Categories," in *How God Became Jesus*, 123–30.

divinity, and the New Testament authors are quite clear about this. Angels do not create, but it is clear that in some of the earliest biblical texts we have, Jesus does create (e.g., 1 Cor 8:4–6; Col 1:15–20). Angels are not to be worshipped, yet Jesus is worshipped in the early church (e.g., Hebrews 1; Rev 1:4–5; 19:10; 22:8–9). What is more, in Greco-Roman contexts a deified emperor is at the bottom of any pyramid scheme; but clearly for the early Christians (if for the moment we can stick with Ehrman's analogy), Jesus is at the very top. Though kings and Moses can sometimes be related to the divine, this is not the same thing as being fully divine and worthy of worship.

Bird aptly draws on both Hurtado and Bauckham to summarize this important point: "A sharp line was drawn between the veneration of intermediary figures and the worship of the one God (so Hurtado), and this was based on the fact that such beings were not part of God's divine identity (so Bauckham)."[59] These scholars are not infallible and have some minor disagreements between them. Yet their body of scholarship suggests that belief in and worship of Jesus as God (with a big "G") were not inspired by pagan demi-gods or angelic beings (who devout Jews and the New Testament authors insisted should not be worshipped; rather, they were inspired by Jesus' claims concerning himself, early Christian reflection on Old Testament passages such as Psalms 2 and 110, and Jesus' post-resurrection appearances.

Second, contrary to Ehrman, there is strong evidence that Jesus claimed the prerogatives and identity of God himself. Ehrman's portrait of Jesus gives short shrift to the miracles, actions, and words of Jesus that point to his own divinity. He also does not allow the confessions and worship of Jesus as God by his followers immediately following the resurrection (e.g., Matt 28:17; Luke 24:52; John 20:28) to contribute sufficiently to his picture. Once these parts of our earliest accounts of Jesus' life are cut up with a skeptical scalpel and Ehrman is left with a scaled-down version of Jesus, it's no wonder he lands where he does. Even using the various criteria—which, as mentioned, should only be used

---

[59] Bird, "Of Gods, Angels, and Men," 35.

to verify, not deny—Ehrman makes it seem that a historical case for key scenes is not possible. In fact, however, not only is it possible, it has been done.[60] Yet Ehrman's readers will never know this, because he never mentions it.

The work of the well-known British scholar N. T. Wright, for example, serves as a more helpful guide in understanding Christological development historically with Jesus' Jewish background firmly in place.[61] Rather than pointing to particular verses in the Gospels where Jesus claims to be God, Wright goes deeper, starting with how first-century Jews understood God and the way he acted in the world. Wright surveys passages in Isaiah, as well as referring to 1 Samuel 5–7; Exodus 40; Leviticus 9; and 1 Kings 8, along with postbiblical writings, which leads him to conclude: "There is thus ample evidence that most second-Temple Jews who gave any thought to the matter were hoping for YHWH to return, to dwell once again in the Temple in Jerusalem as he had done in the time of the old monarchy."[62] The Old Testament pictures Yahweh's return as coming through an agent who would be exalted and honored in a way never seen previously.

Next, Wright argues that first-century Jews, as well as the Old Testament itself, talked about God and his activity in several specific ways: Temple, Torah, Wisdom, Logos, and Spirit. He continues, "Now when we come to the Gospels with those given ways of speaking in our heads, we discover Jesus behaving—not just talking, but behaving—as if somehow those five ways are coming true in a new manner in what he is doing."[63]

Thus, Jesus embodies God by acting in ways only Yahweh can behave. In the Synoptic Gospels—Matthew, Mark, and

---

[60] Darrell Bock and Robert Webb, eds., *Key Events in the Life of the Historical Jesus* (Grand Rapids: Eerdmans, 2010), argue this for twelve such events, including especially the Jewish examination scene, which exhibits a high Christology; see pp. 589–667. This work is a compendium of a collection of scholars in a work published in one of the most widely known international monograph series on the NT (WUNT).

[61] N. T. Wright, *Jesus and the Victory of God* (Minneapolis: Fortress, 1997). For a helpful summary of his argument concerning the deity of Jesus in *Jesus and the Victory of God*, see N.T. Wright, appendix to *There Is a God*, by Antony Flew (New York: HarperCollins, 2007), 188–95; and Marcus Borg and N. T. Wright, *The Meaning of Jesus: Two Visions* (New York: Harper, 1999), 157–68.

[62] Wright, *Jesus and the Victory of God*, 623.

[63] Wright, "Appendix B," in *There Is a God*, 190–91.

Luke—Jesus' teaching points to his role as the Word. For instance, Jesus speaks as One who has authority in himself, moving beyond Old Testament laws by explaining their deeper meaning and their orientation to Jesus the Messiah. In the parable of the Wise Man, Jesus affirms that the one who acts on his words is wise. Jesus presents himself as the Temple and as the One with authority who can forgive sins. And Jesus casts himself as the One who lives by the Spirit. Wright concludes,

> So what we see is not so much Jesus going around saying, "I am the Second Person of the Trinity. Either believe it or not." That really isn't the way to read the Gospels. Rather, reading them as first-century historians, we can see that Jesus is behaving in ways that together say: this whole great story about God who comes to be with his people is actually happening. Only it isn't through Wisdom and the rest. It's in and through the person of Jesus. The fact that draws all of this together is that many Jews in Jesus' day believed that one day Yahweh, the God of Israel, would come back in person to live within the Temple.[64]

In another piece of evidence for the Gospels' commitment to truth, the Gospels universally portray the disciples as failing to understand Jesus' claim to divinity. Instead, Jesus' followers are depicted as slow to perceive the magnitude of Jesus' claims (e.g., Mark 6:52; 7:18; 8:33). Not until after Jesus' death, burial, and resurrection did the disciples—the primary eyewitnesses—begin to understand fully what Jesus was declaring by his actions and words.

All this does not deny that through further theological contemplation the Gospel of John makes the divinity of Christ more explicit than the other Gospels.[65] Certainly, some development existed in the articulation of Jesus' divinity in the early church, but such development is not illegitimate. As D. A. Carson explains,

---

[64] Ibid., 192.
[65] See Andreas J. Köstenberger and Scott R. Swain, *Father, Son, and Spirit: The Trinity and John's Gospel*, New Studies in Biblical Theology (Downers Grove: InterVarsity, 2008), chap. 1.

this development between the Synoptics and John's Gospel points to commonalities that can be observed:

> The Christological distinctiveness of John's Gospel should not be denied, it should not be exaggerated. . . . The Synoptics, for all their portrayal of Jesus as man, portray him as the one who has the right to forgive sins (Mk 2:1–12 par.—and who can forgive sins but God alone?), and relate parables in which Jesus transparently takes on the metaphorical role most commonly assigned to God in the Old Testament. . . . The Synoptic Gospels present in seed form the full flowering of the incarnational understanding that would develop only later; but the seed is there, the entire genetic code for the growth that later takes place.[66]

Third, it is implausible that New Testament authors would have included contradictory Christologies side by side in the same book. This suggests these ideas are related by the biblical authors to each other and not seen as competing, lesser, or greater. For instance, within Paul's letters, the Gospel of John, 1 John, and Hebrews, both exaltation and incarnational Christologies sit side by side. A few examples will demonstrate this.[67]

- John 1:1 affirms that "the Word was God" and then later in the same prologue John 1:14 says, "The Word became flesh and took up residence among us."
- Colossians 1:19 gives us what Ehrman thinks is completely different from earlier exaltation Christologies: "God was pleased to have all His fullness dwell in Him." Yet later, in Col 2:12, Paul refers to the exaltation of Christ when God "raised Him from the dead."
- Or consider how the words in italics in the opening verses of Hebrews include both of what Ehrman claims are contradictory Christologies: "Long ago God spoke to the fathers

---

[66] D. A. Carson, *The Gospel According to John* (Grand Rapids: Eerdmans, 1991) 57.

[67] These examples are drawn from Charles E. Hill, "Paradox Pushers and Persecutors," in *How Jesus Became God*, 178–80.

by the prophets at different times and in different ways. In these last days, He has spoken to us by His Son. God has *appointed Him heir* of all things and *made the universe through Him.* The Son is *the radiance of God's glory* and the exact expression of His nature, sustaining all things by His powerful word. After making purification for sins, He sat down at the right hand of the Majesty on high. So *He became higher in rank than the angels,* just as the name *He inherited is superior to theirs"* (Heb 1:1–4).

Despite the fact that these biblical authors are comfortable placing emphasis on and, apparently, assuming different aspects of Christ's divinity within the same book, Ehrman insists that when he finds these differences they must be understood as evidence for contradictory and evolutionary development. Ehrman's evolutionary theory might have some initial plausibility if these differences were seen *only in different books.* But the fact that these differences are in the *same books* makes his theory problematic to say the least.

Fourth, Ehrman either misinterprets or fails to engage with several very important passages. Space requires we limit ourselves to three examples.

- In Ehrman's chapters on the nature of Jewish monotheism, he never mentions the Shema. Deuteronomy 6:4–5 reads: "Listen, Israel: The LORD our God, the LORD is One. Love the LORD your God with all your heart, with all your soul, and with all your strength." Tilling points out, "It is the closest thing Second Temple Judaism has to a creed, and it remains central to the monotheistic convictions of Jews and Christians alike. . . . This is like talking about British politics during the Second World War, and forgetting to ever mention Winston Churchill."[68] The centrality of this passage in first-century Judaism is why the majority of scholars affirm a strict line between God and everything else.

- Ehrman fails to deal adequately with several key passages in the Gospels. Ehrman argues that neither in Matthew nor in Luke is Jesus seen as preexistent prior to his birth, but

---

[68] Tilling, "Problems with Ehrman's Interpretive Categories," 128.

instead becomes divine—in some lesser sense of the word. According to Ehrman, the Gospel of Mark also does not view Jesus as preexistent and puts his "adoption" even later than the other Synoptics, at his baptism. He interprets Mark in this way because there is no account of the virgin birth, and he sees the voice of God at Jesus' baptism as marking a declaration that during this event Jesus is becoming the Son of God (Mark 1:11). However, as Simon Gathercole points out, God says something similar in Mark 9:7, but clearly Jesus is not being adopted again: "It is hard to see how the voice at the baptism could refer to God's adoption of Jesus and the similar-sounding voice at the transfiguration could mean something different."[69] In a key scene in the Synoptics (Matt 26:62–66; Mark 14:61–64), Jesus claims he will sit with God in heaven, appealing to Psalm 110:1 (as well as Dan 7:13–14 in Matthew and Mark). The Jewish leaders accused Jesus of blaspheming because this was a claim to be equal to God, and they did not believe he could make this claim. This is equivalent to claiming divinity—and the leaders got the point.[70] Also, Ehrman's attempt to understand Mark 2:1–6 as "Jesus claiming a priestly prerogative, but not a divine one"[71] fails because the scribes' outcry was not, "How could he claim to be a priest?" but instead, "He's blaspheming! Who can forgive sins but God alone?" (Mark 2:7). Ehrman also ignores the multiply attested "I have come" texts in the Synoptics, which point to a mission where he is sent from beyond (Mark 2:17; Matt 9:13; Luke 5:32; Matt 5:17; Luke 12:49; Matt 10:34; Luke 12:51; Matt 10:35; Mark 10:45; Matt 20:28). These also point to a view of pre-existence.[72]

• In his reading of Paul, Ehrman has to discount the texts that indicate Jesus was the Creator and equate him with

---

[69] Gathercole, "What Did the First Christians Think about Jesus?," 99. Drawing from his larger monograph on the topic, Gathercole argues from the "I have come" statements for the pre-existence of Jesus in all the Synoptics (97–98).

[70] On this, see Darrell L. Bock, *Blasphemy and Exaltation in Judaism and the Final Examination of Jesus*, WUNT (Tübingen: Mohr-Siebeck, 1998), which is another important work Ehrman fails to engage in his study.

[71] Ehrman, *How Jesus Became God*, 127.

[72] Gathercole, "What Did the First Christians Think about Jesus?," 97–98.

God.[73] For instance, in 1 Corinthians 8:6 the Shema (Deut 6:4–5) is recast so that the one "Lord" and one "God" now reference the Father as "God" and Jesus Christ as the "Lord." And this all takes place in the context where Paul argues adamantly against idolatry! Ehrman claims Paul understands in Philippians 2:6–11 Jesus to be an angel who "is not the Father himself, since it is the Father who exalts him. And he is not—most definitely not—'equal' with God before he becomes human."[74] First, we know of no one who actually claims that Jesus was the Father. This is either a straw man or just a bit of sloppiness on Ehrman's part. Second, among other expressions in Philippians undermining Ehrman's claim that Christ was an angel is Philippians 3:8 where Paul speaks of "knowing Christ Jesus my Lord."[75] Third, Paul includes Jesus as sharing in God's glory and references sections from Isaiah 40–55, which include verses such as Isaiah 42:8: "I am Yahweh, that is My name; I will not give My glory to another or My praise to idols."[76]

Finally, Ehrman confusingly attempts to presuppose his Christological paradigm and then uses that paradigm to prove his evidence. One of the things Ehrman does not state is that while there are many passages scholars have deemed pre-literary, much of this pre-Pauline material indicates incarnational Christologies that could easily be dated at or prior to material he labels as containing exhalation Christologies. However, he places these incarnational pre-Pauline materials chronologically *after* the exaltation Christologies. What evidence does he give to suggest these pre-Pauline incarnational materials come later chronologically? None whatsoever. He simply presupposes his paradigm and then inserts the material on a chronological timeline in a way that is convenient for his proposed paradigm. Nevertheless, presuppositions don't count as evidence. Charles Hill has given more detailed

---

[73] In this paragraph we have summarized many of the points from Chris Tilling, "Misreading Paul's Christology: Problems with Ehrman's Exegesis," in *How God Became Jesus*, 144–48.

[74] Ehrman, *How Jesus Became God*, 263.

[75] Tilling, "Misreading Paul's Christology, Problems with Ehrman's Exegesis," 145.

[76] Ibid., 146.

evidence in support of this conclusion, but a couple of examples will have to suffice here.[77]

Ehrman presents 1 Corinthians 15:3–5 and Romans 1:3–4 as examples of exaltation Christology where Jesus became divine after his resurrection. It is not until later in the book that he presents the pre-literary traditions of Philippians 2:6–11 and 1 Corinthians 8:6. We agree with Ehrman that these two passages present incarnational Christologies. However, Ehrman makes the jump to conclude these were later than the passages with exaltation Christology. How is Ehrman able to draw this conclusion? Hill appropriately challenges Ehrman's entire paradigm on this point: "How do we know that the 'exaltation' traditions are not in fact simply *abbreviations* of fuller incarnational tradition, used to stress Jesus' humanity or his suffering or his fulfillment of prophecies about the coming Messiah? This is surely how they functioned for Paul, as abbreviations of a fuller Christology."[78]

Now you are in a position to better understand why we started off responding to this claim with our discussion about the way in which Ehrman approaches history. The only way he can draw the above conclusion is to have a predetermined chronology that moves from lower to higher Christology. Yet this is where Ehrman's entire paradigm crumbles as unhistorical, for

> . . . if this is predetermined, how is it "historical" and "scientific," open to testing and falsification? Here is where the naturalistic assumption makes a *determinative* difference in historical research. For this presupposed theory of christological development determines all of Ehrman's historical/ theological judgments throughout the book. And so, the problem of a rigidly applied but unproven chronology of belief about Jesus forms a crack that extends throughout his historical reconstruction of early developments in Christology.[79]

---

[77] Hill, "Paradox Pushers and Persecutors?," 181.
[78] Ibid., 182.
[79] Ibid., 183–84.

In summary, our position is that Jesus was not a mere man who became God only later; in Jesus, God took on humanity in the person of Jesus of Nazareth. Within a short decade or two, the early Christians understood that Jesus' identity was intrinsic to the identity of Israel's God and that he was not a second or lesser god but part of God's own being and identity and thus a fitting object of worship. Also, the types of Christology Ehrman claims as contradictory are found side by side, even intertwined, in individual New Testament books such as John's Gospel or Colossians. Apparently, these authors held both views simultaneously without considering them contradictory! This calls Ehrman's alleged trajectory from exaltation to incarnation Christologies into question. For his thesis to be correct, many New Testament authors would have to be internally conflicted.

The rapid rise of Christianity and the fact that large numbers of Christians were prepared to die for their faith are best accounted for by the historical reality of the resurrection of Jesus—not faith in hallucinatory visions of a risen Jesus. This is true especially when one considers that there is no real Jewish precedent to arrive at these conclusions apart from a genuine impetus. The short interval between Jesus' crucifixion and documented worship of Jesus as divine is best explained by Christ's own claim and actions pointing to deity prior to his violent cross-death and then his resurrection.[80]

From Credulity to Skepticism

N. T. Wright offers a helpful critique of the hermeneutic of suspicion that epitomizes Ehrman's approach:

> The guild of New Testament studies has become so used to operating with a hermeneutic of suspicion that we find ourselves trapped in our own subtleties. If two ancient writers agree about something, that proves one got it from the other. If they seem to disagree, that proves that one or both got it wrong. If they say an event or saying fits a prophecy, they made it up to look like that.

---

[80] See "Conclusion: Reasons to Believe" for more on the evidence for Jesus' resurrection.

If there are two accounts of similar events, they are a "doublet" (there was only one event); but if a single account has anything odd about it, there must have been two events, which are now con-flated. And so on. Anything to show how clever we are, how subtle, to have smoked out the reality behind the text. . . . Suspicion is all very well; there is also such a thing as a hermeneutic of paranoia. Somebody says something; they must have a motive; they must have made it up. Just because we are rightly determined to avoid a hermeneu-tic of credulity, that does not mean there is no such thing as appropriate trust, or even readiness to suspend disbelief for a while, and see where it gets us.[81]

Ehrman's journey serves as a reminder that when approach-ing history, we must avoid two extremes: credulity and skepticism. Perhaps surprisingly, one often leads to the other. Bart Ehrman claims to have started his study of the Bible as a fundamentalist but through a painful process left fundamentalism in the wake of his exposure to critical scholarship. In this chapter we have seen that he might not have purged himself of all of his fundamentalist assumptions.[82] Certainly, in many ways Ehrman is the antithesis of a fundamentalist. Nevertheless, his rigid requirements for what the New Testament *must* adhere to in order to be considered true ironi-cally bears striking resemblance to his fundamentalist beginnings.

Discussion Questions

1. How do presuppositions impact the conclusions a person reaches concerning the reliability of the Bible?
2. Explain the difference between legitimate and illegitimate diversity.

---

[81] N. T. Wright, *Meaning of Jesus*, 18.
[82] Daniel Wallace emphasizes this point in "The Gospel According to Bart: A Review of *Mis-quoting Jesus* by Bart Ehrman," *Journal of the Evangelical Theological Society* 49 (2006): 333.

3. What makes harmonization of historical accounts a legitimate exercise?
4. What are some reasons that would lead one to believe that while the Gospels are different, they are not contradictory?
5. What are the problems with the argument that Jesus' divinity was a late development in Christian theology?

Chapter Three

ARE THE BIBLICAL MANUSCRIPTS CORRUPT?

Claims Addressed
---

1. We don't have the original New Testament manuscripts. We only have copies of copies of copies, so we have no idea if what we now have is what the original manuscripts said.

2. While many variants [differences] in the New Testament manuscripts are insignificant, in many cases the likely original reading is highly disputed, and the most likely rendering affects core theological beliefs.

3. There are more variants in the New Testament manuscripts than there are words in the entire New Testament.

4. Early Christians did not have the means to copy texts accurately.

5. Orthodox scribes intentionally changed Scripture at such a high doctrinal level that it is impossible to know for certain if an early scribal corruption has occurred in transmission.

6. It is useless to say the Bible is the inspired Word of God when we don't have the original words.

How Much Evidence Is Enough?

B art Ehrman's beliefs make him skeptical toward the likelihood of the miraculous. Yet in light of his *New York Times* best seller, *Misquoting Jesus*, on—of all things—textual criticism, perhaps he should reconsider. We live in a popular culture where reality shows, YouTube videos, Facebook posts, and tweets are some of the most common forms of entertainment, none of which exactly build patience, attention span, or the ability to investigate details. One would not normally think a book that introduces a discipline that demands painstaking attention to detail, the ability to read languages that most people have never even heard of, and years of research in ancient manuscripts would have an appeal to a lay audience—especially not today. That Ehrman's book on textual criticism has found such a sizable audience in this culture perhaps proves that miracles do exist after all.

At least part of the reason for the attraction of *Misquoting Jesus* is that Ehrman explains how we actually got the Bible that sits in our pews and on our shelves. Despite the fact that the Bible is the most popular book ever produced, many people have never even thought about how the Bible was passed down to us. Most people, including even conservative Christians, don't think the Bible just magically fell from the sky in twelve-point Times New Roman font, in English, full of colorful maps, and bound with a leather cover. Nevertheless, there has been an unfortunate lack of awareness of the most basic facts about the Bible's transmission (i.e., the process by which the Bible has been preserved over the centuries). Likely, part of the reason people have not thought deeply (or at all) about how the Bible was transmitted is that we live well after the invention of Gutenberg's printing press. Nowadays, if someone is working on a writing project and wants to make some copies, it's as easy as putting the paper down and pressing the little button that says "copy." Because of this, you can be confident that this book is, as you read it, exactly like the original from which it was copied. However, making copies has not always been as straightforward, and copyists have not always reproduced the originals as precisely.

In the ancient world copies were made by hand. If you wanted something copied, you didn't buy a copy machine or head down to your local office services store; you hired a scribe. But no matter how careful the scribe, occasional mistakes would happen. You only have to take your favorite book and begin copying portions by hand to see that reproducing an original flawlessly over longer periods of time requires considerable concentration and skill; even then, minor (or not so minor) errors will likely occur sooner or later. You may suffer a momentary lapse of concentration and skip a line, duplicate a word or misspell it, or when you come to a familiar passage reproduce it from memory rather than copying the wording that is on the page in front of you. And these few suggestive examples don't even begin to exhaust all the possibilities of how copying errors might creep in. Add to this the fact that scribes in the ancient world may have copied a manuscript by *hearing it read*, rather than *seeing it*, and sources of error further multiply.

Therefore, with the thousands of copies (called manuscripts) of the New Testament that we have, scholars make comparisons in order to see where changes have been made to the text at different stages in its transmission.[1] Scholars call these changes "variants." Textual criticism is the field of research that studies the various ancient manuscripts to evaluate the different manuscripts and their variant readings to determine which reading is closest to the original. In doing so, text critics consider both the external and the internal evidence. *External* evidence refers to the respective readings in the available manuscripts; *internal* evidence has to do with the way a given variant fits in the context of a particular passage.

When assessing the *external* evidence, a scholar is likely to ask questions such as: What is the date of a given manuscript? Generally, the older the manuscript, the more likely it reflects the original reading (though it of course also matters how many times a manuscript was copied). However, how early a manuscript is produced is not always the most significant piece of evidence. Papyrus, which was the material of the earliest New Testament manuscripts, was susceptible to damage from various weather conditions; over time it often became brittle and crumbled into powder. It was because of these issues that copies had to be updated and recopied. Therefore, if the manuscript it came from is reliable and the scribe does a good job, then the copy is reliable even though it is not necessarily the earliest copy. On the whole, witnesses "are to

---

[1] For a succinct introduction to textual criticism, see Bruce M. Metzger, *A Textual Commentary on the Greek New Testament*, 2nd ed. (New York: UBS, 1994), 1*–16*. The following discussion roughly follows Metzger's presentation on pages 11*–14*.

be weighed rather than counted," that is, determining the original reading of a given passage is primarily a matter of assessing the *quality* of attestation rather than the mere *quantity* (i.e., number of manuscripts that attest to a given reading).

When it comes to *internal* evidence, text critics generally prefer the more difficult reading on the premise that it is more likely that a scribe would have tried to smooth out a reading rather than introduce a difficulty. Scholars also tend to prefer the shorter reading because they believe that, as a rule, scribes would have added words for explanatory purposes (i.e., paraphrase) rather than eliminate words that were in the text in front of them. Thus, scribes might have replaced an unfamiliar term with a more common one or tried to streamline the syntax, such as adding a pronoun or a conjunction.

What is more, when assessing *internal* evidence, text critics take a close look at the style and vocabulary of a given author, say, the Gospel of John, in seeking to determine which of a number of variant readings is most likely what John originally wrote. For example, in John 1:18, did John write that Jesus was "the only God" (*monogenēs theos*) or "the only Son" (*monogenēs huios*)? In terms of intrinsic probability, Bruce Metzger summarizes the judgment of the translation committee of the United Bible Societies version of the Greek New Testament as follows: "A majority of the Committee regarded the reading *monogenēs huios*, which undoubtedly is easier than *monogenēs theos* [note the principle of the "more difficult reading" here] to be *the result of scribal assimilation to Jn 3.16, 18; 1 Jn 4.9*."[2] That is, scribes in all probability conformed the original reading in John 1:18 to the way these other passages in John's Gospel and Letters read. This is but one of a myriad of examples where text-critical work proceeds along a series of carefully formulated principles in order to identify the most likely original wording.

This is no doubt informative and likely interesting to some, but clearly its explanation of textual criticism can hardly explain the success *Misquoting Jesus* has had in today's popular culture.

---

[2] Ibid., 169. The original Greek font was transliterated in this quote. Emphasis added.

Instead, the skeptical conclusions Ehrman draws from his study have likely generated the attention. For example, Ehrman writes,

> If God had inspired the original words, we don't have the original words. So the doctrine of inspiration was in a sense irrelevant to the Bible as we have it, since the words God reputedly inspired had been changed and, in some cases, lost. . . . The only reason (I came to think) for God to inspire the Bible would be so that his people would have his actual words; but if he really wanted people to have his actual words, surely he would have miraculously preserved those words, just as he had miraculously inspired them in the first place. Given the circumstance that he didn't preserve the words, the conclusion seemed inescapable to me that he hadn't gone to the trouble of inspiring them.[3]

Ehrman's work has grabbed the attention of multitudes because the implications are obvious: if he is correct, we have no reason to have confidence that what we are reading is what the original authors really wrote, and the traditional Christian belief in the inspiration of Scripture is undermined.

In this chapter you will see that Ehrman's interpretation is born out of an unduly skeptical approach that stands in direct conflict with many other scholars in the field and even some of his own conclusions. Ehrman himself admits that we have more manuscripts of the Bible than any other piece of literature from antiquity but nonetheless denies its reliability. (Ehrman actually denies the reliability of any book from antiquity as well.)[4] In view of this

---

[3] Bart D. Ehrman, *Misquoting Jesus: The Story Behind Who Changed the Bible and Why* (San Francisco: Harper, 2005), 211.

[4] In *The Reliability of the New Testament*, Ehrman said, "The question is then how can we decide what anybody in the ancient world said. We can't. We wish we could. It would be nice if we could. You would like to think that because you can go to the store and buy an edition of Plato that you are actually reading Plato, but the problem is that we just do not have the kind of evidence that we need in order to establish what ancient authors actually wrote." Robert Stewart, *The Reliability of the New Testament: Bart Ehrman and Daniel Wallace in Dialogue* (Minneapolis: Fortress, 2011), 47.

skepticism, we find ourselves wondering: how much textual evidence would be enough for Ehrman to believe the text of the New Testament is sufficiently reliable? We have over 5,500 Greek manuscripts. Would 8,000 be enough? Or 10,000? The New Testament boasts numerous remarkably early manuscripts compared to other similar ancient literature. What if we had many more early manuscripts? How many would be enough for Ehrman? And how early would be early enough for Ehrman? Indeed, "one gets the impression that no matter what the evidence is, it would not change the outcome. The bar always seems to be set just a bit higher than wherever the evidence happens to be—like the Greek myth of Sisyphus who thought he had finally done enough to push the boulder to the top of the hill only to find it rolled back down again."[5]

The Text of the New Testament: Is It Reliable?

Claim 1:   *We don't have the original New Testament manuscripts. We only have copies of copies of copies, so we have no idea if what we now have is what the original manuscripts said.*

We know all ancient literature by way of copies, not by way of originals. In this way the New Testament is no different. But the New Testament is different from all other ancient literature in that it is *by far* the best-attested book in antiquity. Ancient manuscripts of any kind are difficult to come by. After all, we are talking about writings that are hundreds if not thousands of years old. Textual critics want as many manuscripts as possible in order to compare readings and then determine the correct wording. This is, of course, more difficult with some ancient texts than others because of the quantity and quality of manuscripts available. Consider the numbers of manuscripts that exist for some significant works of antiquity:

---

[5] Andreas J. Köstenberger and Michael J. Kruger, *Heresy of Orthodoxy: How Contemporary Culture's Fascination with Diversity Has Reshaped Our Understanding of Early Christianity* (Wheaton: Crossway, 2010), 210–11. See further the discussion under the heading "The Danger Is in the Ditches" below.

- The works of the Roman historian Tacitus were written in the first century, and we have three manuscripts.
- The *Institutes* by Gaius was written in the second century, and we have three manuscripts.
- The *History of Rome* was written in the first century by Velleius Paterculus, and we have only one manuscript.
- The *Jewish War* by the Jewish historian Josephus is from the first century, and we have fifty manuscripts.[6]

Compared to the number of manuscripts we have of other significant texts of the first and second centuries, having fifty manuscripts of Josephus's *Jewish War* seems pretty impressive. However, in comparison to the New Testament, fifty manuscripts is only a drop in the bucket. Amazingly, we have over 5,800 surviving manuscripts![7] What is more, we have innumerable citations of New Testament manuscripts by way of the writings of Christian teachers in the early church.[8] In fact, these citations are so numerous that Bruce Metzger and, yes, Bart Ehrman have declared that these citations "would be sufficient alone for the reconstruction of practically the entire New Testament."[9]

The New Testament not only has more manuscript evidence than any other book from a similar time period, it also has the smallest time gap between surviving manuscripts and original manuscripts of any work of antiquity. The smaller the gap between the originals and the copies in our possession, the more confident we can be that we have the original words. Consider some of the

---

[6] For further examples, see "Table 1.1: Extant Copies of Ancient Works," Andreas J. Köstenberger, L. Scott Kellum, and Charles L. Quarles, *The Cradle, the Cross, and the Crown: An Introduction to the New Testament* (Nashville: B&H Academic, 2009), 34.

[7] Though, of course, not all of them are complete.

[8] Some have argued that the "free" nature of many of the church fathers' scriptural citations indicates their copies had many variations and were highly unstable. However, Charles Hill ("'In These Very Words': Methods and Standards for Literary Borrowing in the Ancient World," in Charles E. Hill and Michael J. Kruger, eds., *The Early Text of the New Testament* [Oxford: Oxford University Press, 2012], 261–81), has correctly pointed out that there was considerable flexibility with regard to citations in ancient culture. He shows that it was only by the late second century that literal citations became more of a standard as Christian texts were more widely available, leading to an environment that was more conducive for the verification of citations.

[9] Bruce M. Metzger and Bart D. Ehrman, *The Text of the New Testament: Its Transmission, Corruption, and Restoration*, 4th ed. (New York: Oxford University Press, 2005), 86.

following gaps between the originals and the earliest manuscripts we have of ancient literature:

- Our earliest manuscripts of Tacitus's work date to the ninth century, almost 800 years after it was written.
- The earliest useful manuscripts of Josephus's *Jewish War* are from the tenth century and later, nearly 900 years after the original.[10]
- The earliest copy of *History of Rome* was from the eighth or ninth century, which was around 800 years after the original was produced. However, this earlier copy was lost and now exists only in a sixteenth-century copy.
- The best manuscript for Gaius's *Institutes* is from the fifth century, approximately 300 years after the autograph.

These wide gaps are what we have come to expect in the manuscripts available to us of the ancient classics. Yet, once again, the New Testament manuscripts are in a league of their own. Our earliest New Testament fragment, $\mathfrak{P}^{52}$, is a portion of John (specifically, parts of John 18:31–33 on one side and parts of verses 37–38 on the other, having to do with Jesus' trial before Pilate) and is dated approximately AD 125.

The New Testament itself was written between AD 50 and AD 90. So our earliest manuscript dates to only about thirty-five years after the last book of our New Testament was actually written. Though $\mathfrak{P}^{52}$ is the earliest, we have many more manuscripts from the second through the fourth centuries. Codex Sinaiticus, our earliest complete manuscript of the New Testament, comes from the fourth century.[11] The relatively small temporal gap means

---

[10] There is a single manuscript of *Jewish War* from the third century, but it is practically illegible and is only a small fragment of the whole.

[11] The following list gives some of our earliest New Testament manuscripts:
- $\mathfrak{P}^{52}$: manuscript of John from around AD 125 (John 18:31–33, 37–38)
- $\mathfrak{P}^{90}$: manuscript of John from the second century (John 18:36–19:7)
- $\mathfrak{P}^{104}$: manuscript of Matthew from the second century (Matt 21:34–37, 43, 45?)
- $\mathfrak{P}^{66}$: manuscript of John from the late second century
- $\mathfrak{P}^{98}$: manuscript containing Revelation 1 from the second century
- $\mathfrak{P}^{4}$, $\mathfrak{P}^{64}$=$\mathfrak{P}^{67}$: manuscripts containing Luke 1–6 and Matthew 3; 5; 26 from the late second century
- $\mathfrak{P}^{46}$: manuscript of most Pauline epistles from approximately AD 200 (Romans 5–6; 8–16; 1–2 Corinthians; Galatians; Ephesians; Philippians; Colossians; 1 Thessalonians; and

it is unlikely that the textual tradition could have been radically changed during the intervening period without there being evidence for changes visible in the manuscripts we have available to us today. In other words,

> if a particular manuscript of a New Testament
> book (say, Mark) had been changed by a scribe
> in the late first century or early second century, it
> is unlikely that the change would have been able
> to replace the original reading quickly enough so
> that our third- and fourth-century copies of Mark
> would fail to preserve the original text at all (thus
> creating a situation where we would not even
> know the text had been changed).[12]

This is an exceedingly important point that Ehrman, in his written and oral comments, routinely overlooks or glibly dismisses. Ehrman regularly argues that we don't know what the *original* text said; all we know (if that) is what the *earliest available* text says. In fact, he (dubiously) claims that the entire guild of text critics has changed its aim from recovering the original text to restoring the earliest available one. But Ehrman can do this only by a massive and illegitimate argument from silence, claiming a high likelihood that the earliest available text differs significantly from the original text. He makes this argument by magnifying the import of the time gap between the earliest available manuscripts and the date when the New Testament manuscripts were originally written and then asks, "Who knows what happened in the interim?"

In this context, the above-quoted rebuttal by Köstenberger and Kruger that "it is unlikely that the change would have been able to replace the original reading quickly enough so that our third- and

---

Hebrews [grouped with the Pauline corpus])

$\mathfrak{P}^{103}$: manuscript containing Matthew 13–14 from approximately AD 200

- $\mathfrak{P}^{75}$: manuscript containing Luke 3–18; 22–24 and John 1–15 from approximately AD 200–225
- Codex Sinaiticus: manuscript of the entire New Testament from the fourth century; Sinaiticus is our oldest complete manuscript of the New Testament
- Codex Vaticanus: manuscript from the fourth century that contains most of our New Testament (Gospels, Acts, Paul, General Epistles).

[12] Köstenberger and Kruger, *Heresy of Orthodoxy*, 211.

fourth-century copies of Mark would fail to preserve the original text at all (thus creating a situation where we would not even know the text had been changed)" is exceedingly important and even compelling. What Ehrman is arguing is not merely that significant changes might have crept in immediately after the writing of the original text; what he is saying is, not only did those changes creep in massively and immediately, there is no trace of the changes in even the earliest manuscripts we have.

That, we submit, is undue skepticism (coupled with a dose of conspiracy theory). Ehrman's claim is we have lost traces of the original because of the changes. He has no way of knowing this. It is more likely that we *have* the changes *and* the original in our manuscript tradition since we have so many other copies. In other words, we have *too much* of the text, not *too little*. We could well say that it is more likely that our problem is that we have *105 percent* of the text, not that we have *lost some* of it.

Claim 2:   *While many variants [differences] in the New*
Testament manuscripts are insignificant,
in many cases the likely original reading
is highly disputed and the most likely
rendering affects core theological beliefs.

In *Misquoting Jesus*, Ehrman is particularly interested in surveying the most significant variants, apparently in order to call into question the reliability of the New Testament. He writes,

> In some instances, the very meaning of the text is at stake, depending on how one resolves a textual problem: Was Jesus an angry man [Mark 1:41]? Was he completely distraught in the face of death [Heb 2:8–9]? Did he tell his disciples that they could drink poison without being harmed [Mark 16:9–20]? Did he let an adulteress off the hook with nothing but a mild warning [John 7:53–8:11]? Is the doctrine of the Trinity explicitly taught in the New Testament [1 John 5:7–8]? Is Jesus actually called "the unique God" there [John 1:18]? Does

the New Testament indicate that even the Son of
God himself does not know when the end will
come [Matt 24:36]? The questions go on and on,
and all of them are related to how one resolves difficulties in the manuscript tradition as it has come
down to us.[13]

Several responses are in order concerning these specific examples listed by Ehrman. First, Ehrman seems to want to have his
cake and eat it too. On the one hand, in the previous quote and in
much of *Misquoting Jesus,* he seems to want to leave the impression that we don't really have a clue what the original text said.
On the other hand, Ehrman is confident he has determined which
reading is the earliest, as you can readily see once you read his
explanation of the textual evidence.

Second, in three of these cases, almost all evangelical scholars
and translations would agree with Ehrman. Most modern Bibles
exclude the variant trinitarian formula found in a small number
of manuscripts for 1 John 5:7–8 ("For there are three that testify in
heaven: the Father, the word, and the Holy Spirit, and these three
are One") due to the manuscript evidence against such a reading.
The story of the adulterous woman in John 7:53–8:11 and the
long ending of Mark (16:9–20) are widely bracketed off in modern translations with a textual note indicating that the passages
are not found in the earliest manuscripts. In other words, these
variants are not highly disputed. Most textual critics—no matter
their theological commitments—are in agreement over the earliest readings in these cases, and this is made clear in most modern
Bible translations. For Ehrman to suggest that the original wording of Mark 16:9–20; John 7:53–8:11; and 1 John 5:7–8 is a matter
of debate and contention among scholars (whether conservative
or otherwise) is therefore inaccurate at best and disingenuous at
worst; these three passages should be removed from his list of
alleged problems with the New Testament witness.

Third, in the other four examples, different textual critics have
come to different conclusions. This is not the place to get into the

---

[13] Ehrman, *Misquoting Jesus,* 208.

technicalities of the arguments; and while Ehrman's proposals are far from conclusive, for the sake of argument, let's assume he is correct.

- If Mark were depicting Jesus as being angry in Mark 1:41, this would not be the only place where the New Testament portrays Jesus as angry or indignant (see, e.g., Matt 21:12; 23:13–36). The Bible in no way equates all anger with sin, so this does not cause a major theological problem, no matter which reading is adopted.

- What is the theological significance, if Ehrman is correct, of Hebrews 2:8–9 depicting Jesus as distraught in the face of death? According to Ehrman, the author of Hebrews "repeatedly emphasizes that Jesus died a fully human, shameful death, totally removed from the realm whence he came, the realm of God. His sacrifice, as a result, was accepted as the perfect expiation for sin. Moreover, God did not intervene in his passion and did nothing to minimize his pain. Jesus died 'apart from God.'"[14] But as Dan Wallace has pointed out, "If this is the view of Jesus throughout Hebrews, how does the variant that Ehrman adopts in 2:9 change that portrait?"[15] Ehrman's argument undercuts itself.

- No matter if Jesus is called "only God" or "only Son" in John 1:18, both readings still fit well within the Gospel of John and the rest of the New Testament. With regard to Jesus' deity, John opens his Gospel by affirming that "in the beginning was the Word, and the Word was with God, and the Word [later identified as Jesus, see John 1:14,17] was God," and he closes the Gospel with Thomas's confession of Jesus as "My Lord and my God!" (John 20:28). With regard to Jesus' unique sonship, this is clearly affirmed in passages such as John 1:14 or John 3:16 and 18 where no significant textual variants exist.[16]

---

[14] Bart D. Ehrman, *The Orthodox Corruption of Scripture: The Effect of Early Christological Controversies on the Text of the New Testament* (Oxford: Oxford University Press, 1993), 149.

[15] Daniel Wallace, "The Gospel According to Bart: A Review Article of *Misquoting Jesus* by Bart Ehrman," *Journal of the Evangelical Theological Society* 49 (2006): 339.

[16] Note that in this case we may see the opposite of what Ehrman calls the "orthodox

- Since Mark 13:32 includes Jesus' comment about the Son of Man not knowing when the end will occur, there is no textual problem if Ehrman is right and Matthew 24:36 indicates the same thing. Ehrman may have a theological problem with Jesus confessing that even he, during his earthly sojourn, was not aware of the timing of his return, but this is a separate issue from casting doubt on our ability to know what the original wording of a given New Testament statement was.

In summary, the point here is not that the reader should be unconcerned with what the original text actually said in the cases in question. Ehrman is right to argue that these variants are important—what the original text actually said does matter. However, Ehrman is wrong to give the impression that, depending on the variant reading chosen, there is some kind of irresolvable problem for the Bible. As we have seen, in several cases he adduces a reading that virtually all scholars, conservative and otherwise, agree is secondary. In other cases, even if Ehrman's reconstructed wording is correct, there is no problem because a given textual assertion is also found in other places in the New Testament and no real theological contradiction or incongruity exists.

Sometimes one gets the impression that Ehrman believes simply by casting doubt on the New Testament's reliability he has already proven his case. Not so—he and others like him should listen to the way his (in many cases legitimate) concerns can be answered; if the answer is satisfactory, there is no more legitimate reason for doubt. Otherwise, the problem is not with the actual textual data but with the unfounded skepticism of agnostics such as Ehrman. Unless a skeptic such as Ehrman is willing to engage in genuine dialogue with scholars on the other side, his struggle is only an exercise in solipsism (a conversation with himself) rather than an actual interchange with others in search for possible explanations. This makes one wonder whether Ehrman is really as open to the evidence as he claims to be. Instead, it seems that he *wants*

---

corruption" of Scripture—scribes changing the reading "God" to "Son." On the "orthodox corruption" of Scripture, see further the discussion of claim 5 below.

doubt to have the last word simply because he is committed to doubting the reliability of Scripture rather than believing it.

As with other areas we have considered, we see a problem with Ehrman's exaggerating the significance of the issues he raises. The slant put on things is always tilted in the direction of doubt—even when other answers do exist that do not lead to the conclusions he makes about the Scripture being problematic.

Claim 3:   *There are more variants in the New Testament manuscripts than there are words in the entire New Testament.*

This has become one of Ehrman's standard one-liners used in various media appearances and debates. He often also adds that there are somewhere between 200,000 to 400,000 variants in our manuscripts. These numbers can overwhelm someone unacquainted with the field of textual criticism, but they mean little. Here's why.

First, as the response to claim 1 has made clear, we have an embarrassment of riches when it comes to New Testament manuscripts; no other piece of literature in antiquity even comes close. Most see this overwhelming amount of evidence for the New Testament manuscripts as positive. The more manuscripts we have, the more comparisons can be made by scholars to determine with higher probability the original words of the earliest manuscripts. Naturally, the more manuscripts we have, the more variants we have, because copyists made errors in copying. The large number of variants is actually a testimony to how much evidence we have. However, Ehrman turns this advantage into a negative. The more manuscripts are available, there will inevitably be more variants; Ehrman chooses to emphasize the number of variants rather than the number of manuscripts.

Mark Roberts provides an illustration to help us better understand what the number of variants really means for our assessment of the reliability of the New Testament:

> This book [that Roberts has written] has almost
> 50,000 words. Suppose I asked two people to make

copies of this book by hand. Suppose, further, that they made one mistake every 1,000 words (99.9 percent accuracy). When they finished, each of their manuscripts would have 50 mistakes, for a total of 100. This doesn't sound too bad, does it? But suppose I asked 2,000 people to make copies of my book. And suppose they also made a mistake every 1,000 words. When they finished the total of mistakes in their manuscripts would be 100,000. This sounds like a lot of variants—more than the words in my book, Bart Ehrman would say. But in fact the large number of variants is a simple product of the large number of manuscripts.[17]

Or consider another hypothetical situation. Suppose we only had one manuscript of the New Testament. Of course, in this case we would have no variants, and Ehrman could not shock an unsuspecting public with such numbers; yet this would hardly be a better situation. One could imagine what a skeptic would say if we had only one, or say even ten, New Testament manuscripts: "We don't have enough manuscripts to be sure what the original wording was!" Of course, as almost any textual critic would tell you, having thousands of New Testament manuscripts is a *good* thing. It is important to realize that "due to the vast number of manuscripts, the challenge of textual criticism is a different one than we might expect—it is not that we are *lacking* in material (as if the original words were lost), but rather we have *too much* material (the original words, plus some variations). When it comes to reconstructing the original text of the New Testament, that latter position is much preferred over the former."[18]

Second, the overwhelming majority of New Testament variants are minor and insignificant. Most of the variants are spelling errors, nonsense readings that are easy to spot, meaningless word

---

[17] Mark D. Roberts, *Can We Trust the Gospels? Investigating the Reliability of Matthew, Mark, Luke, and John* (Wheaton: Crossway, 2007), 33–34.

[18] Köstenberger and Kruger, *Heresy of Orthodoxy*, 209.

order changes, or Greek article changes that make no difference in English translations. Ehrman himself at times has to admit this is indeed the case. For example, he writes, "To be sure, of all the hundreds of thousands of textual changes found among our manuscripts, most of them are completely insignificant, immaterial, and of no real importance of anything other than showing the scribes could not spell or keep focused any better than the rest of us."[19] So if most of these thousands of variants are insignificant, why does Ehrman keep making statements about the number of changes being greater than the number of words in the New Testament? It makes for a nice sound bite, to be sure, but it does little to bring clarity to the discussion.

Claim 4:   *Early Christians did not have the means to copy texts accurately.*

Ehrman paints the picture of the earliest Christian scribal community as kind of like the Wild West: there was no infrastructure; there were no norms; and there was no organization in how things were done. According to Ehrman, the earliest Christian scribes copying the texts were not professionals, could sometimes not even read themselves (or were barely able to read), and were clearly more susceptible to grievous mistakes. This alleged instability in the earliest centuries of transmission in part gave rise to Ehrman's cynicism toward the possibility of actually knowing the words of the original manuscripts. The question at stake is this: Did early Christianity have the scribal infrastructure to reliably copy the books of the New Testament? Ehrman says no. However, several lines of evidence appear to challenge this conclusion.

First, the handwriting found in the earliest Christian manuscripts indicates that most of the earliest scribes were professional scribes trained in copying both documentary and literary texts.[20] Indeed, most of these scribes would not have been literary scribes who would have primarily copied books to be sold commercially. However, these early Christian scribes would have been well trained for employment by individuals to do such things

---

[19] Ehrman, *Misquoting Jesus*, 207.

[20] For more on handwriting and ancient scribes see Köstenberger and Kruger, *Heresy of Orthodoxy*, 186–90.

as copy letters, reproduce formal literary pieces, write letters by taking dictation, and generate administrative documents. These multifunctional scribes were prevalent in the first century. One doesn't have to wonder if the earliest Christians used such scribes. In the New Testament Tertius is identified as such a scribe who was employed by Paul: "I Tertius, who wrote this letter, greet you in the Lord" (Rom 16:22). Moreover, there is no reason to conclude that scribes like Tertius were less skilled than scribes who were used primarily for commercial copying. Harry Gamble, in a study on earliest Christian texts, has noted, "There is no reason to think that commercially produced books were of higher quality than privately made copies. Indeed, frequent complaints suggest they were often worse."[21]

Second, the use of *nomina sacra* (lit., "sacred names," abbreviations for common words denoting deity such as "God" or "Lord"; see further below) and the codex suggests that the early church was better organized and more sophisticated in its copying practices than Ehrman gives it credit. The *nomina sacra*, as mentioned, are abbreviations of special words such as *Jesus, Christ, Lord*, and *God* in early Christian documents. It is unclear where exactly this practice originated, but we do know that *nomina sacra* were *not* used as simple abbreviations to save space—the primary reason abbreviations are used today. There are much longer words in Greek than "God" or "Jesus" or any of the other words abbreviated, and it would make little sense to choose to shorten these words in order to save space. Instead, these words were likely abbreviated to express reverence and devotion. In any case, these abbreviations are significant because they appear in the earliest manuscripts, are exclusive to Christianity, and are widespread across regions and languages. This means that early Christian scribes were not simply making things up as they went but had a "degree of organization, of conscious planning, and uniformity of practice . . . which we have hitherto had little reason to suspect."[22]

---

[21] Harry Y. Gamble, *Books and Readers in the Early Church* (New Haven, CT: Yale University Press, 1995), 91.

[22] T. C. Skeat, "Early Christian Book-Production," in *The Cambridge History of the Bible*, vol. 2 (Cambridge: Cambridge University Press, 1969), 73.

The widespread use of the codex in the early church also points to a more formal scribal infrastructure than that assumed by Ehrman. In the early days of Christianity, most in the Greco-Roman world were using the scroll, which was made from papyrus or parchment. Writing was done on the inside of the scroll, which was rolled out to be read and then rolled back up for storage. The codex, on the other hand, looks more like our modern-day books. It was made by taking a stack of papyrus or parchment, folding it in half, and then binding everything together. While the rest of the culture was still primarily using scrolls, Christians preferred using the codex, and its use was a widely established Christian practice by at least the early second century. The codex was likely used because of its ability to hold more than one book so that collections of writings, such as the four Gospels and Paul's letters, could be bound together. The rest of the Greco-Roman culture did not begin to prefer the codex to the scroll until sometime in the fourth century. The upshot for our purposes is that "the dominant use of the codex, like the *nomina sacra*, reveals a Christian scribal culture that is quite unified, organized, and able to forge a new literary path by employing a revolutionary books technology that would eventually come to dominate the entire Greco-Roman world."[23]

The codex suggests that a mentality developed early on that certain books belonged together and were held in high regard. This means care would have been given to how they were copied. This is not to say copies were perfect (as we already noted) or that scribes never made corrections because of what they thought the text should read (that is for reasons of doctrine). Nevertheless, this is not a great problem since the number of manuscripts we have allows us to see what an array of copyists have done so we can spot when such changes were likely made. That leads to our next point.

The topic of early Christian scribal infrastructure is obviously a specialized field of research, and we have only provided a brief response to Ehrman's argument. There are gaps in our knowledge about how texts were transmitted, but this is the nature of history. Nevertheless, the use of multifunctional professional scribes,

---

[23] Köstenberger and Kruger, *Heresy of Orthodoxy*, 195.

nomina sacra, and the codex directs us away from thinking of the early transmission of Christian texts as the Wild West and more like a developing colony: an infrastructure was in place, established norms existed, and organization was evident.[24]

Claim 5: *Orthodox scribes intentionally changed Scripture at such a high doctrinal level that it is impossible to know for certain if an early scribal corruption has occurred in transmission.*

Ehrman admits that most changes in New Testament manuscripts are inconsequential, but a central argument in *The Orthodox Corruption of Scripture* and *Misquoting Jesus* is that there was an intentional and widespread orthodox corruption of manuscripts in order to weaken the arguments of those Christian scribes viewed as heretics. In some cases this was likely the case. Nevertheless, Peter Williams points out that Ehrman actually does not prove what he sets out to establish:

> Although Ehrman's sound bite the "Orthodox Corruption of Scripture" has been widely received, he has in fact demonstrated how little deliberate corruption went on. The number of examples of deliberate corruption which he alleges is rather limited, and we must remember that Ehrman brings these examples together from *all* manuscripts. Without even allowing for the fact that many of his examples may in fact be wrong, it is amazing to find so few cases even of possible deliberate corruption when searching across so many manuscripts. Thus Ehrman's own research

---

[24] For more on the significance of the codex and *nomina sacra* and their implications for early Christian scribal infrastructure, see Scott Charlesworth, "Indicators of 'Catholicity' in Early Gospels Manuscripts," in Hill and Kruger, eds., *Early Text of the New Testament*, 37–48. He concludes, "The combination of evidence adduced here shows that conventional textual practices were *already established* among 'catholic' Christians *by the second half of the second century* when standard-sized codices of the canonical gospels were being produced for public use in Christian gatherings" (p. 48, emphasis added).

shows how overwhelmingly scribes did not seek deliberately to change the text.[25]

Neither Williams nor we are denying that *some* scribes, for a variety of reasons, felt free to alter the text in the manuscript they were copying. Yet, as Michael Kruger has concluded after surveying the early Christian testimony concerning the scriptural status of these texts and the scribes' approach to transmitting them,

> Although we have no reason to think the text in the unobservable stages was being transmitted only with strict fidelity, we also have no reason to think it was being transmitted only with wild and unbridled textual alterations. The matrix of early Christian attitudes toward textual reproduction suggests that *we should expect no greater level of textual diversity in the earliest stages than we find preserved in our current manuscript tradition.*[26]

Moreover, to argue for the large-scale corruption Ehrman claims, he must assert that he cannot only be confident that he knows *what* changes were made but also *why* they were made. The irony of such confidence, in view of his skepticism regarding our inability to recover the wording of the original manuscripts, is palpable.

Two questions, then, are in order concerning Ehrman's thesis that this intentional orthodox corruption was widespread. First, how can Ehrman be so sure he knows what the later corruption was if we are not able to get back to what the original, in all probability, actually said?[27] Once again, Ehrman's argument seems to be contradictory.

---

[25] P. J. Williams, "Ehrman's Equivocation and the Inerrancy of the Original Text," in *The Scripture Project: The Bible and Biblical Authority in the New Millennium*, ed. D. A. Carson, 2 vols. (Grand Rapids: Eerdmans, forthcoming).

[26] Michael J. Kruger, "Early Christian Attitudes on the Reproduction of Manuscripts," in Hill and Kruger, eds., *Early Text of the New Testament*, 80 (emphasis added).

[27] Similarly, Charles E. Hill and Michael J. Kruger, "Introduction: In Search of the Earliest Text of the New Testament," observe: "Indeed, it is only when we can have some degree of assurance regarding the original text that we are even able to recognize that later scribes occasionally

Second, how can Ehrman be so sure he knows what a scribe was thinking? It is difficult enough to determine the thoughts of a writer when an abundance of information exists telling us about a person's background, context, and overall theology. Yet we know next to nothing about the particular scribes who copied the texts. All we have is the text they copied, but for Ehrman this is enough to consistently claim he knows what the scribes who copied these texts were thinking. Ehrman completely lacks confidence in determining the original wording but has abundant confidence in his ability to decipher the thoughts of scribes about whom he knows little! Robert Stewart wisely suggests caution:

> Still, there is nothing that says one *cannot* identify the theological reason behind a significant textual variant. I am proposing, however that one proceed with caution and a bit of reasoned skepticism on this point, recognizing that equally possible alternative theories [other than Orthodox scribes changing the text] may arise. Indeed, fairminded text critics and early church historians frequently interpret the same data in differing ways. Therefore, one should hold one's conclusions in this regard with a fair amount of epistemological humility.[28]

In fact, Ehrman combines this widespread "orthodox corruption of Scripture" theory with his larger theory that there was an early and pervasive orthodox conspiracy to get rid of all equally legitimate but competing forms of Christianity.[29] Once this larger theory, out of which Ehrman is working, is understood, it is easier to comprehend why his impulse is so strong to assign sinister motives to scribes. These confident conclusions are likely more due to Ehrman's larger theory than the actual clarity of the evidence

---

changed it for their own theological purposes. Without the former we would not have the latter" (ibid., 5).

[28] Robert Stewart, "Why New Testament Textual Criticism Matters: A Non-Critic's Perspective," in *Reliability of the New Testament*, 9–10.

[29] For more on Ehrman's larger theory concerning early Christianity, see chapter 4.

concerning motivations on the part of particular ancient scribes. However, as already suggested, even if Ehrman were correct in all his examples of widespread orthodox tampering with the text (which is unlikely), his conclusions would have little impact on the larger question of our ability to recover the original words since his argument depends on being able to locate the earlier reading.

Claim 6:   *It is useless to say the Bible is the*
              inspired Word of God when we
              don't have the original words.

In recounting his own testimony, Ehrman explains, "I kept reverting to my basic question: how does it help us to say that the Bible is the inerrant word of God if in fact we don't have the words that God inerrantly inspired, but only the words copied by the scribes—sometimes correctly but sometimes (many times!) incorrectly?"[30]

No scholar claims we have the original manuscripts (the so-called biblical "autographs") of the New Testament. However, acknowledging that we no longer have the *autographs* is different from saying we no longer have the *words of the original manuscripts*. It is also different from arguing there never was an original we can pursue. Just because we don't have the original doesn't mean we can't work back to determining what it said, given how many copies we have. Textual criticism always worked with this premise from its inception. Ehrman has demonstrated that there are differences (known as variants) in the copies, but no one disputes this point. For Ehrman to prove we no longer have the words of the originals, he would need to show that none of the variants in the available manuscripts (i.e., copies) go back to the original. Ehrman has demonstrated that particular manuscripts have been altered at certain points, but he has nowhere demonstrated that, among the thousands of manuscripts available to scholars today, the original words have utterly vanished.

As Peter Williams has pointed out, "It might be correct to say that such and such a scribe in history 'did not have' the divinely

---

[30] Ehrman, *Misquoting Jesus*, 7.

given words, but this cannot be converted into a statement about what 'we' have."[31] Referring to the same statement from the Ehrman quote that began this response, Williams goes on to observe, "The phrases 'we don't have the words that God inerrantly inspired, but only the words copied by the scribes' introduces a rather strange dichotomy. After all, these words are generally the same. Since it is the words that are inspired, not the ink, words do not lose inspiration by being copied."[32] Ehrman fails to make a distinction between the *material* entity of the original *manuscripts* and the *immaterial* original *words* that were written on the autographs. Not having the original *manuscripts* is different from not having the original *words*.

Ehrman hardly makes an attempt to demonstrate that we don't have the "original words." Instead, he opts to make his argument by way of a theological claim. For example, Ehrman writes,

> The only reason (I came to think) for God to inspire the Bible would be so that his people would have his actual words; but if he really wanted people to have his actual words, surely he would have miraculously preserved those words, just as he had miraculously inspired them in the first place. Given the circumstance that he didn't preserve the words, the conclusion seemed inescapable to me that he hadn't gone to the trouble of inspiring them.[33]

And later:

"If God really wanted people to have his actual words, surely he would have miraculously preserved those words, just as he had miraculously inspired them in the first place. Given that he didn't preserve the words, the conclusion must be that he hadn't gone to the trouble of inspiring them."[34]

---

[31] Peter Williams, "Review of Bart Ehrman, *Misquoting Jesus*," http://evangelicaltextualcriticism.blogspot.com/2005/12/review-of-bart-ehrman-misquoting-jesus_31.html.

[32] Ibid.

[33] Ehrman, *Misquoting Jesus*, 211.

[34] Ibid.

Ehrman's argument can be broken down into three propositions:[35]

1. If God had inspired the New Testament autographs, he would have either provided us with the originals or prevented any corruption in the transmission.
2. The New Testament autographs no longer exist, and the available manuscripts are corrupt.
3. Therefore, God did not inspire the New Testament autographs.

However, why should one believe proposition 1? Ehrman thinks this is how God would have inspired the New Testament autographs, or at least this is how Ehrman would have done it. But the Bible does not teach that proposition 1 is true, nor does it logically follow. We are aware of no ancient Christian doctrine that claims proposition 1. The proposition seems logical to Ehrman, but "*seeming* logical is not the same thing as *being* logical."[36] Again, Peter Williams aptly rebuts Ehrman's logic:

> Must all people have all of God's word at every moment for it to be possible to believe that God "wanted people to have his actual words"? Or will it suffice to believe that God wanted some people to have some of his words for some of the time? Just what are the conditions that Ehrman is demanding for inspiration to be logical? He does not say. Ehrman's whole emphasis here, however, is on human reception. Yet there is no need for reception of the whole of God's word by the entire human race for it to function as his word. God may speak through a single verse that someone encounters, or through a single book of the Bible that has been translated into a particular language. Similarly, for us to insist on a perfectly printed version of the Bible bound under a single cover

---

[35] For similar breakdown of propositions see Stewart, "Why New Testament Textual Criticism Matters," 11.
[36] Ibid., 12.

before we can believe that the text is inspired is a
rather anthropocentric condition. We would also
be insisting that scripture could only be verbally
inspired for us in the twenty-first century if God
fulfilled for us conditions that could not possibly have been fulfilled for Christians prior to the
invention of printing. It is not irrational to suppose that God has not made his word available
to all people at all times and places. Yet it is possible to maintain that in our time and place the
whole original words of the New Testament are
available in a relatively limited number of Greek
witnesses.[37]

In summary, Ehrman causes confusion by not clearly distinguishing between the original *autographs* and the original *words*.
Christians believe the *words* written in the original autographs
were inspired, *not* the material entity (i.e., the specific piece of
papyrus or parchment we call an "autograph"). In other words,
we don't need the original *manuscript* in order to have the original *words*.

No one who practiced textual criticism when it began or for
decades afterward doubted there was an original to pursue. They
also were confident some readings were not original (something
one cannot claim unless he or she has a good suspicion about what
the original was). I (Bock) once had a discussion with someone
who made a claim about the lack of originals that Ehrman makes.
I asked him, "When you preach Acts, do you preach manuscript D
[Codex Bezae, a later copy that contains many longer expansions
of the shorter original text of Acts]?" He replied, "No." "Why?" I
asked. He replied, "Because it is not original." I responded, "That
is my point. There is a difference between having the original and
working to determine what it was likely to have been because you
are confident an original existed."

Ehrman has produced little to no evidence that we no longer
have the original words in the manuscripts available to us today. In

---

[37] Williams, "Review of Bart Ehrman, *Misquoting Jesus.*"

the end he relies on a theological argument insisting on how God would have inspired the New Testament autographs if he had in fact done so (something Ehrman himself denies). Claiming inspiration to be false because "if I were running things, I would have done things differently" is a far cry from a sound textual or theological argument.

The Danger Is in the Ditches: Absolute Certainty and Absolute Despair

We return to the question posed at the beginning of this chapter: How much evidence would be enough for Ehrman to trust the reliability of the New Testament? At a forum Ehrman was posed this very question. He responded this way:

> Well, if we had early copies, if we had copies of Mark . . . suppose next week, there is an archaeological find in Egypt, say, it's in Rome, an archaeological find in Rome, and we have reason to think that these 10 manuscripts that are discovered were all copied within a week of the original copy of Mark, and they disagree in 0.001% of their textual variation, then I would say, that's good evidence, and that's precisely what we don't have.[38]

This response demonstrates that Ehrman is not living in the real world of historical inquiry. Ehrman's requirements for reliability are so far beyond what is available for any ancient work that, if Ehrman is correct, all historical research in antiquity is utterly doomed. In other words, he is using a standard no one in classics uses for those sets of texts—even as he claims to be using approaches that are a part of generally practiced, solid historical method.

Ehrman has admitted that the Bible has the best manuscript evidence for any ancient book; alas, this is not enough for him. His response to the above question demonstrates that Ehrman's

---

[38] "Can We Trust the Text of the New Testament? A Debate Between Daniel B. Wallace and Bart D. Ehrman" (Saturday, October 1, 2011; DVD; Dallas: Center for the Study of New Testament Manuscripts, 2011).

skeptical conclusions are the result of an underlying disposition of doubt rather than reasonable conclusions drawn from the actual evidence. Of course, Ehrman does not see it like this. He often chides others who disagree with his conclusions as having their own theological agendas while presenting himself as the unbiased historian.[39] Yet, as Dan Wallace has noted, despite Ehrman's brilliance, "His biases are so strong that, at times, he cannot even acknowledge them."[40]

Ehrman asks, "How can we decide what anybody in the ancient world said?" and answers his own question by concluding, "We can't."[41] However, despite Ehrman's evident skepticism, when turning to the task of writing about Jesus and the early church, Ehrman himself assumes the sufficient certainty of the New Testament. Recently, Ehrman has written a book called *Did Jesus Exist?* where he argues, against a small group called "mythicists," Jesus did in fact exist. Throughout the book Ehrman rightly defends the historical existence of Jesus, but his arguments are based on the assumption that we can actually know what the New Testament authors said. He reconstructs a historical Jesus using primarily the words of the New Testament Gospels. He would not be able to make such arguments if he did not trust (at least in a general and significant way) the transmission of the New Testament. What is more, as pointed out earlier in this chapter, one of Ehrman's central points in *Misquoting Jesus* is that scribes at times intentionally changed the text; Ehrman can make such an argument only by assuming that he can know with some degree of confidence what the original text actually said.

So, on the one hand, it seems that even Ehrman has more confidence in the transmission of the text than it sometimes appears. But on the other hand, Ehrman often still insists on taking an all-or-nothing approach: one must either be absolutely certain or be absolutely cynical about the reliability of the transmission of the New Testament. This black-and-white, either-or approach once again

---

[39] For instance, see Bart D. Ehrman, *Did Jesus Exist? The Historical Argument for Jesus of Nazareth* (San Francisco: HarperOne, 2013), 5–6, 336–39.

[40] Wallace, "Gospel According to Bart," 349.

[41] This is a response to a question recorded in *The Reliability of the New Testament*, 47.

resembles more the categories of a rigid fundamentalist than Ehrman seems to realize. It appears as if Ehrman, in his journey from fundamentalism to agnosticism, has jumped from one extreme to the other, from absolute certainty to utter skepticism. Here we have seen that since Ehrman cannot be absolutely certain about every single textual variant, he declares that we cannot know much of anything about what the original authors wrote. But in view of the arguments of this chapter, the question is not so much if we can have *absolute* certainty but if can we have *sufficient* certainty in the reliability of the New Testament transmission. The answer to this question is a resounding yes; we *can* have sufficient certainty in the text of the New Testament.[42] If the question is posed in this way, and answered in the affirmative, we avoid the ditches on either side of the road and find the reasonable answer at the center, the road on which even Ehrman himself, perhaps surprisingly, likes to travel in many of his writings.[43]

Discussion Questions

1. Describe how scholars weigh the evidence when determining the original words of the New Testament.
2. Explain why there are so many variants in the manuscripts of the New Testament.
3. Discuss how the passages that have legitimate cases for alternate readings might have an impact on one's overall theology.
4. Why is it misleading when critics claim that since we do not have the words the original New Testament authors wrote, God did not inspire Scripture's words?

---

[42] See, e.g., Paul D. Wegner, *Journey from Texts to Translations: The Origin and Development of the Bible* (Grand Rapids: Baker, 2004).

[43] See Wallace, "Gospel According to Bart."

Chapter Four

WERE THERE MANY CHRISTIANITIES?

Claims Addressed
---

1. The German scholar Walter Bauer's book *Heresy and Orthodoxy in Earliest Christianity* was "the most important book on the history of early Christianity to appear in the twentieth century. . . . The argument [made by Bauer] is incisive and authoritative, made by a master of all the surviving early Christian literature."

2. Writings from equally early and legitimate "heretical" forms of Christianity do not currently exist because they were destroyed by the proto-orthodox in the first century.

3. Early Christianity was wildly diverse, with no group having a legitimate claim to the "true" form of Christianity.

4. You can never rely on the winners to write an unbiased account of the past. The New Testament is unified because the winning "orthodox" party got to choose what was in its canon.

5. No standards were in place during the earliest stage of Christianity to distinguish correct from incorrect teachings concerning the person and work of Jesus Christ.

6. Second- and third-century orthodox leaders were innovators rather than guardians of tradition, creating what is now known as orthodoxy.

7. Orthodoxy, which was the product of much later church councils, did not exist in the first century: "For example, none of the apostles claimed

that Jesus was 'fully God and fully man,' or that he was 'begotten not made of one substance with the Father,' as the fourth-century Nicene Creed maintained. The victorious group called itself orthodox."

8. The creation of a canon was one of the strategies used by the proto-orthodox to diminish the authority of other early Christian literature.

The Power of Cherished Beliefs

Sometimes people want something to be true so badly they believe in it even though the facts point in the opposite direction. We remember the disappointment we felt as children when we were told Santa Claus was not real. We wanted Santa and all the magic that filled a seven-year-old's mind about Santa to be true, but eventually we reached the point where we realized the evidence just wasn't there. At times Bart Ehrman treats people who believe in the Bible as if they were small children who, wanting to hold onto the magic of the stories they grew up hearing in Sunday school, believe even when the historical evidence doesn't back up their belief. Ehrman describes his own development from conservative Christianity to its more liberal form to his current agnosticism as a heroic (or at least an honest, mature) attempt to look at the evidence objectively. In contrast to his own journey for truth, he suggests that those who have confidence in the Bible are simply sticking their heads in the sand and are not really considering the evidence, or at least not objectively. After all, if they were really willing to examine the evidence objectively, they would come to the same conclusions he does! This attitude is apparent when Ehrman describes the evangelical students in his university classes as those who "cover their ears and hum loudly so that they don't have to hear anything that might cause them to doubt their cherished belief."[1]

While Ehrman may unfairly stereotype Christians, his caricature highlights a legitimate concern: those who place their faith in a grand narrative must be open to engage any detailed countervailing evidence that seems to cast doubt on the truthfulness of what they have become accustomed to believe; if at closer scrutiny these

---

[1] Bart D. Ehrman, *Jesus, Interrupted: Revealing the Hidden Contradictions in the Bible (And Why We Don't Know About Them)* (San Francisco: HarperOne, 2009), 14.

doubts turn out to be well founded and evidence to support one's beliefs is lacking, the honest person ought to stop putting faith into what they know is untrue—just like most children eventually stop believing in Santa Claus.

When it comes to the origins of historic Christianity, Ehrman believes that in the first century there was no such thing as Christianity (in the singular) as a coherent, widely agreed-upon set of beliefs, but only Christiani*ties* (in the plural). All that existed were different versions of Christianity that claimed to be true with equal legitimacy. According to Ehrman, what later became the traditional version of Christianity—now known as orthodoxy—was simply the particular form of the early Christianities that happened to win the political power struggle in the second through fourth centuries of the Christian era. Then this victorious faction proceeded to rewrite history to make it appear they were the only legitimate form of Christianity (he calls this group the "proto-orthodox").[2] In keeping with this narrative, Ehrman alleges that the early days, before the powerful church leaders forcefully asserted their authority and eliminated diversity, should serve as a kind of model for our culture today: "There is instead a sense that alternative understandings of Christianity from the past can be cherished yet today, that they can provide insights even now for those of us who are concerned about the world and our place in it."[3]

---

[2] Incidentally, this makes those of us who adhere to historic Christianity the heirs of forebears who, sometimes brutally, stamped out the beliefs of others, not because they believed their faith was true but because they wanted to protect their positions or power. Thus, it turns out, Ehrman's view is not only one among a plethora of conspiracy theories so prevalent in American culture; it is also exceedingly cynical: Christianity is based on nothing more than beliefs that proved expedient for the powerful, and the actual truth (i.e., religious diversity!) was brutally suppressed by those who knew better. See on this David R. Liefeld, "God's Word or Male Words? Postmodern Conspiracy Culture and Feminist Myths of Christian Origins," *Journal of the Evangelical Theological Society* 48, no. 3 (2005): 449–73. See also Craig A. Blaising, "Faithfulness: A Prescription for Theology," in *Quo Vadis, Evangelicalism? Perspectives on the Past, Direction for the Future: Nine Presidential Addresses from the First Fifty Years of the Journal of the Evangelical Theological Society* (Wheaton: Crossway, 2007), 201–16. The earliest Christian faith was held by people who had no social or political power. In fact, their beliefs were socially unpopular and led to persecution as Tacitus's remark in *Annals* 15.44 or Pliny the Younger's *Letter to Trajan* in the early second century shows. Pliny mentions a group in Bithynia (modern Turkey) who worshipped Jesus as God, clearly a proto-orthodox group. They clung to their "proto-orthodoxy" not because it gave them social-political power but because they believed it was true *despite* their being a persecuted minority. It is important not to ignore these roots to this faith in thinking about the point Ehrman is making.

[3] Bart D. Ehrman, *Lost Christianities: The Battles for Scripture and the Faiths We Never Knew* (Oxford: Oxford University Press, 2003), 257.

In today's world the air we breathe is filled not with the absolute truth claims of Christianity but with a strong scent of postmodernism, which has as one of its foundational truths, ironically, that no one view is true (except, apparently, the view that says no one view is true!). Truth is relative, and all that is left is competing perspectives.[4] This sentiment has become so commonplace in our culture that it is often accepted without much thought. Just as Ehrman has ridiculed evangelical Christians for "covering their ears" to the evidence so they can continue holding to their own cherished beliefs, however, Ehrman's readers should consider the evidence in order to discern whether *Ehrman's* narrative, which happens to fit nicely with the cherished beliefs of many in our *culture*, is supported by the actual historical evidence available with regard to first-century Christianity.

Ehrman's Paradigm

Claim 1: *The German scholar Walter Bauer's book*
           Heresy and Orthodoxy in Earliest Christianity
           was "the most important book on the history of
           early Christianity to appear in the twentieth-
           century. . . . The argument [made by Bauer] is
           incisive and authoritative, made by a master
           of all the surviving early Christian literature."[5]

Ideas do not appear out of thin air, and in order to better understand Ehrman, it is important to understand a little about the origins of Ehrman's theory. Ehrman's paradigm is built on the work of a scholar named Walter Bauer who wrote at the beginning of the twentieth century. In 1934, Bauer, in a work entitled *Heresy and Orthodoxy in Earliest Christianity*, argued that the traditional form of Christianity (i.e., orthodoxy) was actually nothing but the view imposed by one early Christian sect onto the rest of Christendom. In support of this claim, Bauer argued that in certain regions heresy was the original form of Christianity. What is more, he claimed that in certain areas heretical views were at least an established minority.

---

[4] See on this the helpful collection of essays edited by Andreas J. Köstenberger, *Whatever Happened to Truth?* (Wheaton: Crossway, 2005), with suggestions for further reading on pages 137–39.

[5] Ehrman, *Lost Christianities*, 173.

Bauer also asserted that the Roman church's control over certain regions at the end of the second century allowed orthodox groups retrospectively to alter the history of the early church and destroy evidence for early diversity in order to cement their own control over Christendom. Therefore, according to Bauer, traditional Christian theology did not really derive from the teachings of Jesus and his earliest disciples but is merely the view of the Roman church as it crystallized in the fourth through sixth centuries of the Christian era.

Despite Ehrman's belief that Bauer's work is the "most important book on the history of early Christianity in the twentieth century" and that Bauer's argument is "incisive" and "authoritative," the main lines of evidence used by Bauer in support of his thesis have been widely discredited.[6]

The central pieces of Bauer's argument have been referred to as a "constructive fantasy of the author" and "elegantly worked out fiction."[7] Moreover, critics have rightly pointed out that despite the title of his work that suggests he will explore *earliest* Christianity, Bauer has remarkably neglected the earliest available evidence we have—the New Testament documents themselves! Instead of studying these and other first-century documents, Bauer's book is almost entirely devoted to second-century and later works, which he then anachronistically reads back into the first century.[8]

---

[6] For a fuller refutation of the Bauer thesis, see Andreas J. Köstenberger and Michael J. Kruger, *Heresy of Orthodoxy: How Contemporary Culture's Fascination with Diversity Has Reshaped Our Understanding of Early Christianity* (Wheaton: Crossway, 2010), chaps. 1 and 2.

[7] Darrell L. Bock, *The Missing Gospels: Unearthing the Truth behind Alternative Christianities* (Nashville: Thomas Nelson, 2007), 50.

[8] As noted above, scholars have severely critiqued the Bauer thesis from multiple angles. To name just one more specific recent critique, Scott Charlesworth in his article "Indicators of 'Catholicity' in Early Gospels Manuscripts," in Charles E. Hill and Michael J. Kruger, eds., *Early Text of the New Testament* (New York: Oxford University Press, 2012), 237–48, argues that the "catholicity" indicated by the *nomina sacra* and the standardization of Gospel codices calls the Bauer thesis into question: "Did the disparate Gnostic, Montanist, and Marcionite groups who dominated early Christianity reach a consensus about conventional approaches to manuscript production in the second half of the second century? This is highly improbable when each group was busy insisting on its own version of Christianity and when early non-canonical gospel papyri are private manuscripts without indications of catholicity. Non-canonical gospels are also at a serious disadvantage in terms of frequency of citation and preservation. If the 'heterodox' were in the majority for so long, non-canonical gospels should have been preserved in greater numbers in Egypt. But the earliest papyri provide 'no support for Bauer's view'" (pp. 46–47, citing B. A. Pearson, *Gnosticism and Christianity in Roman and Coptic Egypt* [New York: T&T Clark International, 2004], 13–14).

Even Ehrman admits that Bauer's arguments have some major weaknesses.[9]

Yet despite the fact that the evidence for Bauer's thesis has been widely discredited, refuting virtually all his detailed proposals, incredibly, his diversity paradigm lives on.

> What is the secret of this larger-than-life persona that transcends factual arguments based on the available evidence? We believe it is that diversity, the 'gospel' of many in our culture, has now assumed the mantle of compelling truth—and this 'truth' must not be bothered by the pesky, obstreperous details of patient, painstaking research, because in the end, the debate is not about the details but about the larger paradigm—diversity.[10]

Ehrman has kept Bauer's conclusions, but the details of the argument have changed. This raises the question why Bauer's thesis should be considered, as Ehrman has put it, "incisive and authoritative." The examination of the arguments below will make clear that though the Bauer-Ehrman proposal makes for an attractive narrative in the currents of our contemporary culture, anyone who adopts such an account must be firmly committed not to allow the "pesky details" to get in the way of a good story. Perhaps in this case it is actually Ehrman who clings to an old, unproven view when the evidence patently does not hold up. The fact is the magic of Bauer's thesis has long disappeared.

Claim 2:   *Writings from equally early and legitimate*
                "heretical" forms of Christianity do not

---

[9] In *Lost Christianities*, Ehrman writes: "Specific details of Bauer's demonstration were immediately seen as problematic. Bauer was charged, with good reason, with attacking orthodox sources with inquisitional zeal and exploiting to a nearly absurd extent the argument from silence. Moreover, in terms of his specific claims, each of the regions that he examined has been subjected to further scrutiny, not always to the advantage of his conclusions. Probably most scholars today think that Bauer underestimated the extent of proto-orthodoxy and overestimated the influence of the Roman church on the course of the conflicts" (p. 176).

[10] Köstenberger and Kruger, *Heresy of Orthodoxy*, 18.

> *currently exist because they were destroyed*
> *by the proto-orthodox in the first century.*

The problem with this claim is that it is an argument from silence. There is no evidence to support it. It is beyond dispute that outsiders destroyed *Christian* texts during persecutions in the opening centuries of Christianity. There is also evidence that some Christian works were destroyed by *other Christians* in the third century because of their deviant theology. What is not known is whether the earliest Christians destroyed the works of other forms of Christianity, whether they were simply lost, or whether these writings ever existed at all! If anything, the evidence, as you will see below (claim 3), suggests that the heretical groups producing texts in the second and third centuries were either not widespread in the first century or, in some cases, had not even come into existence.

Claim 3:   *Early Christianity was wildly diverse,*
              with no group having a legitimate claim
              to the "true" form of Christianity.

No one disputes that Christianity was filled with controversies in its early days (or in modern days, for that matter). However, in a discussion over the *origins* of Christianity, it makes little difference if there was considerable diversity among groups that labeled themselves Christian in the second, third, or fourth century. The existence of divergent second-century groups proves that diversity existed in subsequent centuries but is not directly relevant since this is not evidence from the days when the church first came into being—the first century. Thus, one of the problems with the Bauer-Ehrman thesis is that it illegitimately presents evidence from the second and subsequent centuries as relevant for the discussion of the origins of Christianity while minimizing the first-century evidence.[11]

---

[11] In my (Bock) introduction classes, I point out that evidence from the first century does not exist for a few of the four diverse groups in the opening chapters of Ehrman's *The New Testament: A Historical Introduction to the Early Christian Writings*, 5th ed. (Oxford/New York: Oxford University Press, 2011). The only first-century evidence we have is for some Jewish groups that embraced Jesus but who questioned the deity of Jesus (the Ebionites). All the other groups noted such as the Gnostics and Marcionites lack first-century sources. So this makes

This, as mentioned, does not mean diversity was absent from first-century Christianity. The New Testament documents themselves indicate there were divergent views. However, these same New Testament documents also stress the importance of holding to true doctrine and denunciating false teachings in no uncertain terms (which presupposes a commonly agreed-upon standard of what was true and what was false teaching).[12] Rhetorically, when Ehrman begins listing heresies of the second and third centuries, it might feel like a powerful argument; in reality it serves only to divert attention from the *central* question, which is what the state of Christianity was in its *earliest* period, that is, the first century. The real question, therefore, is whether the diversity evident in subsequent centuries actually *preceded* the unity which is found at Christianity's origins.

Even if (for argument's sake) the evidence from the second or third century were to show that heretical groups were widespread and stable, this would in no way prove they were *equally* widespread and stable in the first century. In fact, however, the evidence from the second and third centuries points in the same direction as that from the first century: in both cases orthodoxy was more established and stable while heresy was less widespread and unified than Ehrman implies.[13]

Of the various second-century heretical groups, Gnosticism clearly posed the greatest threat to Christianity. So instead of reviewing all the various groups, which has been done elsewhere, we will focus our survey here on what can be known about Gnosticism in comparison with orthodoxy.[14]

---

his key opening claim for diversity in that textbook exaggerated. We also must note that early disputes about practice (circumcision or not as required for Gentiles) which the New Testament notes and about which there was vigorous debate does not touch on the core Christological orthodoxy to which these first-century "proto-orthodox" works also attest.

[12] Paul's letters to the Galatians and Colossians (see esp. Gal 1:6; Col 2:11–21), his Pastoral Epistles to Timothy and Titus (e.g., 1 Tim 1:3; Titus 1:5), as well as 2 Peter, 1 John, and Jude were all written to a significant extent to combat heresy.

[13] See Köstenberger and Kruger, *Heresy of Orthodoxy*, chap. 3, esp. 89–98.

[14] For a survey of the major sects of the second century, see Antti Marjanen and Petri Luomanen, eds., *A Companion to Second-Century Christian "Heretics,"* Supplements to Vigiliae Christianae 76 (Leiden: Brill, 2005). One of the burdens of *The Missing Gospels* by Darrell Bock was to document how deep and widespread these core Christian beliefs were in the early orthodox sources. It surveys the documents before Irenaeus in full and shows a core orthodoxy was present.

To begin with, Gnosticism is actually a label for various diverse religious ideas that never developed into a singular organized movement because the various Gnostic groups only shared a few key similarities. In fact, the singular term "Gnostic" probably does not capture the diversity of groups that carry that label. Most likely, because Gnostics could not agree among themselves, they never formed a church or groups of churches. This lack of organization and unity within Gnosticism stands in stark contrast with orthodoxy. The emphasis on the rule of faith, the early agreed-upon set of core Christian beliefs, demonstrates an early unity in orthodox writings.[15] As early as the AD 40s and 50s, orthodox churches were planted and flourished.[16] Also, as orthodox churches spread, they viewed themselves as part of a unified network of churches (something one writer has dubbed a "holy internet").[17] These churches organized themselves amazingly early, developed a leadership structure, agreed on core beliefs, and interacted with one another.

Also, early orthodoxy had no official authority to suppress what they perceived to be heretical teachings. It was not until AD 313, when Emperor Constantine's Edict of Milan mandated religious toleration, that Christians acquired official means to take action against heretical groups. However, by this time there is no mention of Gnostics, which suggests that Gnosticism was definitively refuted before orthodoxy had any official power to do so. Without an official governing body, the orthodox would have been able to defeat Gnosticism only by its advantage in numbers rather than by a decree of the church.

This evidence from the second and third centuries suggests orthodoxy was much more widespread and unified than the fragmented Gnostic movement. The implication from this evidence concerning Gnosticism is that if the Gnostic movement was the biggest threat to orthodoxy in the second century, the sects that

---

[15] See the response to claim 6 below.

[16] Paul embarked on at least three missionary journeys, commonly dated to the years 47–48, 49–51, and 51–54. See, e.g., Andreas J. Köstenberger, L. Scott Kellum, and Charles L. Quarles, *The Cradle, the Cross, and the Crown: An Introduction to the New Testament* (Nashville: B&H Academic, 2009), 391–94.

[17] Michael B. Thompson, "The Holy Internet: Communication Between Churches in the First Christian Generation," in Richard Bauckham, ed., *The Gospels for All Christians: Rethinking the Gospel Audiences* (Grand Rapids: Eerdmans, 1998), 49–70.

posed considerably less of a threat can likewise not be considered as early or well developed as orthodoxy.

Also, pause to consider this. It is patently absurd to believe that the broad orthodox unity and organization of the second century appeared almost out of nowhere; the most reasonable appraisal of the evidence is that doctrinal unity had early origins (i.e., Jesus and the apostles). By contrast, it appears that heretical movements were less organized and widespread in the second century because they were *parasitic of orthodoxy*.[18] In other words, orthodoxy built its theology around the teachings of Jesus and the apostles while heretical movements borrowed from and then mixed the teachings of orthodoxy with other worldviews to develop their divergent theologies. These heresies were later deviations from orthodoxy rather than equally legitimate claims to the teachings of Jesus and the apostles. In the next chapter we will explore the specifics of these second- and third-century heretical writings in greater detail and see how they were clearly distinguishable from the books of the New Testament.

Claim 4: *You can never rely on the winners to write an unbiased account of the past. The New Testament is unified because the winning "orthodox" party got to choose what was in its canon.*

Ehrman puts the traditional view in a no-win situation. On the one hand, Ehrman argues that the New Testament presents a unified theology because it was "written by the winners" who suppressed all other views. On the other hand, if the New Testament were to include a considerable amount of diversity, this would prove Ehrman right in his belief that early Christianity was unsettled and doctrinally open! The way Ehrman has framed the argument is "heads, he wins; tails, the traditional position loses." This problem is particularly evident in light of chapter 2, where we saw how Ehrman argues that the New Testament is full of irreconcilable differences. The theory that "winners" set out to unify the canon by eliminating diversity seems to contradict the argument

---

[18] Another point in *The Missing Gospels* was to show how varied the Gnostic writings were, lacking as unified a presentation of teaching as early orthodox texts on God, Jesus, and salvation.

for competing theologies within the New Testament canon. Are we to assume that these "orthodox winners," who were crafty enough to use their power to eliminate other, equally valid forms of Christianity, were not competent enough to succeed when attempting to unify the canon? We don't think either of these theories works historically (i.e., the disunity of the canon and the "orthodox winners" choosing the canon), but arguing for *both* of them at the same time certainly seems to defy logic.

Once the assumption that one must be absolutely neutral to write history is allowed to slip into the argument, Ehrman not only places the traditional view in a no-win situation, but demolishes the entire enterprise of history. After all, there is no such thing as an unbiased historian or writer—including Ehrman!

Contrary to Ehrman's assumption, the Greek and Roman historians during the New Testament period believed the ideal eyewitnesses were not dispassionate observers and critics but rather participants in a series of events who were able to draw on their firsthand experience to interpret the significance of these events.[19] Along these lines, D. A. Carson offers a contemporary analogy with regard to John's Gospel, which is applicable to the entire New Testament:

> [T]he Fourth Gospel [i.e. the Gospel of John] can be accepted as what it manifestly purports to be: a reliable witness to the origins, ministry, death, resurrection, and exaltation of Jesus the Messiah. Such a witness does not have to be dispassionate, merely truthful. One accepts, for instance, that the first witnesses of Auschwitz were both truthful and passionate, even if in some circles they were at first easily dismissed because of their passion. But in retrospect, merely dispassionate witness regarding Auschwitz would be obscene. Similarly, a dispassionate witness to the person,

---

[19] Samuel Byrskog, *Story as History—History as Story: The Gospel Tradition in the Context of Ancient Oral History*, Wissenschaftliche Untersuchungen zum Neuen Testament 123 (Tübingen: Mohr-Siebeck, 2000), 64.

teaching and work of Christ would necessarily be profane. To set theological commitment and historical reliability against each other as necessarily mutually incompatible is unrealistic; worse, it is an invitation to profanity.[20]

Indeed, the New Testament writers *were* partial—as they *should have been*—since they believed Jesus really did rise from the dead. Who would *not* be passionate about the story of a friend who was killed publicly only to rise from the dead three days later? More so, who would *not* be zealous if they believed their revered teacher rose from the dead after claiming to be the long-awaited Messiah and Savior of the world? On the basis of this false set of assumptions—that the New Testament was written and ultimately canonized by "the winners" and thus cannot be trusted—Ehrman justifies discounting large portions of the New Testament documents.

Claim 5:   *No standards were in place during the earliest stage of Christianity to distinguish correct from incorrect teachings concerning the person and work of Jesus Christ.*

Once the earliest written evidence we have for Christianity—the documents found in the New Testament—are examined, it becomes apparent that a doctrinal core was used as a standard against heresies in the earliest forms of Christianity.[21] It should also be noted that, at least in part, these works were distinguished from other noncanonical writings because of their early date and connection with Jesus' original followers (who in turn rooted the claims of Christianity in Jesus' fulfillment of Old Testament messianic predictions).[22] The following selection will provide just a sampling of verses that could be offered in response to Ehrman's

---

[20] D. A. Carson, *The Gospel According to John*, Pillar New Testament Commentary (Grand Rapids: Eerdmans, 1991), 40.

[21] See the response in chapter 5 to claim 1 that explains that one of the distinguishing marks of canonical writings was their connection to the apostles, which is what makes the writings included in the canon early and thus so important. The point being made is a historical one, not so much a theological point. These are our earliest sources! In other words, they are cited not because they are New Testament texts but because they provide our earliest historical window into beliefs of the period.

[22] Köstenberger and Kruger, *Heresy of Orthodoxy*, 74–77.

argument (in the case of Paul's letters given in presumed chronological order of writing):[23]

Gospels and Acts

- Matthew 16:16–18: *Simon Peter answered, "You are the
  Messiah, the Son of the living God!" And Jesus responded,
  "Simon son of Jonah, you are blessed because flesh and blood
  did not reveal this to you, but My Father in heaven. And I
  also say to you that you are Peter, and on this rock I will build
  My church, and the forces of Hades will not overpower it"* (cf.
  Mark 8:27–30; Luke 9:18–20; John 6:66–69).
- Matthew 28:18–20: *Then Jesus came near and said to them,
  "All authority has been given to Me in heaven and on earth. Go,
  therefore, and make disciples of all nations, baptizing them in
  the name of the Father and of the Son and of the Holy Spirit,
  teaching them to observe everything I have commanded you.
  And remember, I am with you always, to the end of the age."*
- Acts 2:42: *And they devoted themselves to the apostles'
  teaching, to the fellowship, to the breaking of bread, and to
  the prayers.*

New Testament Letters
Paul:

- Galatians 1:6–9, 11–12: *I am amazed that you are so quickly
  turning away from Him who called you by the grace of Christ
  and are turning to a different gospel—not that there is another
  gospel, but there are some who are troubling you and want to
  change the good news about the Messiah. But even if we or an
  angel from heaven should preach to you a gospel other than
  what we have preached to you, a curse be on him! As we have
  said before, I now say again: If anyone preaches to you a gospel
  contrary to what you received, a curse be on him! . . . Now I
  want you to know, brothers, that the gospel preached by me is
  not based on human thought. For I did not receive it from a*

---

[23] Remember we cite these verses for this point because they reflect the earliest views. It is not
an objection or response to challenge whether one thinks they are true. They *are* evidence for
what these early Christians affirmed and believed.

*human source and I was not taught it, but it came by a reve-
lation from Jesus Christ.*

- 2 Thessalonians 2:15: *Therefore, brothers, stand firm and
  hold to the traditions you were taught, either by our message
  or by our letter.*
- Romans 16:17: *Now I urge you, brothers, to watch out for
  those who cause dissensions and obstacles contrary to the doctrine you have learned. Avoid them.*
- 1 Timothy 1:3: *As I urged you when I went to Macedonia,
  remain in Ephesus so that you may instruct certain people not
  to teach different doctrine.*
- 2 Timothy 1:13–14: *Hold on to the pattern of sound teaching
  that you have heard from me, in the faith and love that are in
  Christ Jesus. Guard, through the Holy Spirit who lives in us,
  that good thing entrusted to you.*

Jude[24] and John:

- Jude 1:3: *Dear friends, although I was eager to write you
  about the salvation we share, I found it necessary to write and
  exhort you to contend for the faith that was delivered to the
  saints once for all.*
- 1 John 4:1–2: *Dear friends, do not believe every spirit, but test
  the spirits to determine if they are from God, because many
  false prophets have gone out into the world. This is how you
  know the Spirit of God: Every spirit who confesses that Jesus
  Christ has come in the flesh is from God.*

These verses paint a different picture than Ehrman's portrait of
an early Christianity that lacked standards to distinguish legitimate
from false teaching. Instead, these passages reveal that the leaders of
the church in the New Testament era, beginning with Jesus' appoint-
ment of twelve apostles and on through Paul and other church
leaders, were instructed and sent out to pass on Jesus' message to
subsequent generations. The importance of remaining faithful to
the teaching of the apostles was continually emphasized. The core

---

[24] Some place the writing of Jude in the AD 50s.

message of the gospel tied to the importance of the nature and work of Christ was defended in view of heretical versions of Christianity.

None other than the apostle Paul, the most towering figure of Christianity in its earliest stages, acknowledged that even he was not free to alter this core apostolic message. To the Galatian church he wrote that "even if we [Paul and his fellow apostles] or an angel from heaven should preach to you a gospel other than what we have preached to you, a curse be on him!" (Gal 1:8). And to the Corinthian church he wrote, "Now brothers, I want to clarify for you the gospel I proclaimed to you. . . . For *I passed on to you* as most important *what I also received*: that Christ died for our sins according to the Scriptures, that He was buried, that He was raised on the third day according to the Scriptures" (1 Cor 15:1, 3, emphasis added). If not even Paul was able to alter the foundational message of Christianity, no one in the early church was allowed to tamper with the core teaching concerning the saving death, burial, and resurrection of the Lord Jesus Christ.

In fact, the early church had ways to pass on core orthodoxy in the early period, even before there was a standard formal collection of New Testament writings. They used the Hebrew Scriptures as their foundational text. They used information provided in doctrinal summaries to pass on core teaching (Rom 1:2–4; 1 Cor 8:4–6; 11:23–25; 15:3–6; numerous texts in the Pastoral Epistles). They used hymns and liturgical portions to affirm core doctrine (Col 1:15–20; Phil 2:6–11). The sacraments or rites of baptism and the Lord's supper also taught key theology. So Scripture, doctrinal summaries, singing, and sacraments taught key doctrines in the core life and worship of the church long before the works of the New Testament were written and used as an authoritative, unified collection.

Claim 6: *Second- and third-century orthodox leaders were innovators rather than guardians of tradition, creating what is now known as orthodoxy.*

The actual evidence indicates that the adherents to orthodoxy in the second century were not innovators but faithful stewards, passing down the theology offered by the apostolic leaders in the

New Testament period. The rule of faith played an important part in maintaining in the church leaders of the second century the essential convictions of Jesus and the apostles. The Rule is found throughout orthodox writings of the second and third centuries from various geographical locations.[25] Though the Rule was never explicitly spelled out by the church fathers, most agree that it served as the core affirmation of the church's common faith.[26] The Rule suggests that from the beginning of the post-New Testament church, a geographically diverse group of writers had a theological standard that unified them. In these second-century leaders' writings, it is evident they saw themselves as handing down these central teachings (e.g., Irenaeus, *Haer. 3.3.3*).

What is more, the second- and third-century orthodox church fathers stressed that their message was rooted in the Jewish Scriptures (i.e., the Old Testament), which were also the Scriptures of Jesus and the apostles. This stands in stark contrast to second-century sects that had no use for the Old Testament and failed to award any authority to it. For the early church, on the other hand, the rule of faith was rooted in the Old Testament prophetic message fulfilled in Jesus and subsequently proclaimed by the apostles. These central teachings were then passed on to the Fathers who saw it as their role to pass on, rather than invent, the apostolic message.

Claim 7:   *Orthodoxy, which was the product of much later church councils, did not exist in the first century: "For example, none of the apostles claimed that Jesus was 'fully God and fully man,' or that he was 'begotten not made of one substance with the Father,' as the fourth-century Nicene Creed maintained. The victorious group called itself orthodox."*[27]

At this point Ehrman is correct but only in part. However, he has created somewhat of a straw man that fails to represent accurately the opposing side and is easily dismantled. One must

---

[25] Ibid., 54.

[26] See the concluding chapter in *The Missing Gospels*, where a survey of these writings shows that almost all of them mention in one way or another what this core theology was.

[27] Ehrman, *Jesus, Interrupted*, 215.

assume that as a seasoned scholar Ehrman is fully aware that mature expressions of Christianity are not claiming that Jesus or the apostles actually uttered the exact words or used the same constructs as the Nicene Creed. This is a bit like saying the doctrine of the Trinity is not in the Bible because the Bible does not use the word *Trinity*. No legitimate argument for or against the Trinity can be made on the sole basis of whether the word *Trinity* is used in the Bible. Neither can one decide if certain later theological statements, such as those found in the Nicene Creed, are faithful to the New Testament simply by saying Jesus and the apostles did not use the exact same language.

Building on the previous response to Ehrman,[28] the question arises: What happened to the Rule of Faith, the core of early Christian belief that was passed on to and argued for by church leaders in the second and third centuries? It is inconceivable to believe that the early church fathers, who took great care to emphasize their roles as "handing down" the tradition, would have scrapped its core tenets in favor of their own novel teachings. In recent works Gerald Bray has convincingly shown that the Rule of Faith was passed on and then made its way into the third- and fourth-century creeds.[29] Bray examined the Nicene Creed step-by-step, tracing each part of the Creed from the New Testament through to the Fathers and then to its codification. However, one must be careful with this point.

It is a mistake to conclude from Bray's work that fourth-century orthodoxy formulated doctrines with the same wording as the New Testament. Yet Ehrman's argument implicitly forces one of two options on the listener: either (1) the fourth-century creeds spoke in the same way as the New Testament, or (2) the creeds are in contradiction with Jesus and the apostles. These fourth-century creeds were formulated in part to deal with then-current controversies that were especially philosophical in nature. This led to fresh expression being given to old teachings to deal with new issues. So maintaining that the Fathers preserved orthodoxy and conveyed it to those who

---

[28] See the response to claim 6.

[29] See Gerald L. Bray and Thomas C. Oden, *Ancient Christian Doctrine*, 5 vols. (Downers Grove: InterVarsity, 2009).

articulated the creeds does not mean the New Testament authors would have conceived their theology in the same constructs as the formulations of the creeds. The creeds are an organic continuation of the theology of the New Testament without any transmutation of the DNA of the New Testament gospel message, which in turn is rooted in the Old Testament.[30] Note, for example, the similarities between Irenaeus, writing in the second century, and what was codified in later creeds, such as the Nicene Creed:

> [The Church believes] in one God, the Father Almighty, Maker of Heaven and earth, and the sea, and all things that are in them; and in one Christ Jesus, the Son of God, who became incarnate for our salvation; and in the Holy Spirit, who proclaimed by the prophets the (divine) dispensations and the coming of Christ, his birth from a virgin, his passion, his rising from the dead, and the bodily ascension into heaven of our beloved Lord Jesus Christ, and his manifestation from heaven in the glory of the Father to sum up all things in one and to raise up again all flesh of the whole human race (Irenaeus, *Haer.* 1.10.1).

> We believe in one God, the Father, the Almighty, maker of heaven and earth, of all that is, seen and unseen. We believe in one Lord, Jesus Christ, the only Son of God, eternally begotten of the Father, God from God, light from light, true God from true God, begotten, not made, of one Being with the Father; through him all things were made. For us and for our salvation he came down from heaven, was incarnate of the Holy Spirit and the Virgin Mary and became truly human. For our sake he was crucified under Pontius Pilate; he suffered death and was buried. On the third day

---

[30] See John Behr, *The Way to Nicea*, The Formation of Christian Theology, vol. 1 (Crestwood, NY: St. Vladimir's Seminary Press, 2001).

he rose again in accordance with the Scriptures; he ascended into heaven and is seated at the right hand of the Father. He will come again in glory to judge the living and the dead, and his kingdom will have no end. We believe in the Holy Spirit, the Lord, the giver of life, who proceeds from the Father [and the Son], who with the Father and the Son is worshiped and glorified, who has spoken through the prophets. We believe in one holy catholic and apostolic Church. We acknowledge one baptism for the forgiveness of sins. We look for the resurrection of the dead, and the life of the world to come (Nicene Creed).

To recap, the orthodox creeds of the fourth and fifth centuries were not imposed onto the early church but were instead logical continuations of New Testament orthodoxy. As a way to see the bigger picture, the following serves as an approximate outline of the relationship between orthodoxy and divergent forms of heresy in the first 300 years of Christianity:[31]

- AD 33: Jesus dies and rises from the dead.
- AD 40s–60s: Paul writes letters to various churches; orthodoxy is pervasive and mainstream; churches are organized around a central message; undeveloped heresies begin to emerge; Scripture, schooling, singing, and sacraments teach core theology along with emerging early orthodox writings circulating in the churches.
- AD 60s–90s: The Gospels and the rest of the New Testament are written and continue to propagate the orthodoxy that preceded them; orthodoxy continues to be pervasive and mainstream; heresies are still undeveloped.
- AD 90s–130s: The New Testament writers pass from the scene; the Apostolic Fathers emerge and continue to propagate the orthodoxy that preceded them; orthodoxy is still

---

[31] Köstenberger and Kruger, *Heresy of Orthodoxy*, 66.

pervasive and mainstream; heresies begin to organize but remain relatively undeveloped.

- AD 130s–200s: The apostolic fathers die out; subsequent Christian writers continue to propagate orthodoxy that preceded them; orthodoxy is still pervasive and mainstream, but various forms of heresy emerge; these heresies, however, remain subsidiary to orthodoxy and remain variegated.

- AD 200s–300s: Orthodoxy is solidified in the creeds, but various forms of heresy continue to rear their heads; orthodoxy, however, remains pervasive and mainstream.

Claim 8:   *The creation of a canon was one of the strategies used by the proto-orthodox to diminish the authority of other early Christian literature.*

In order to explain the historical problems with this argument, we've broken the following response into two sections: "The Concept of Canon" and "The Contents of the New Testament Canon."

The Concept of Canon

Rather than serving as a weapon created by the orthodox church fathers to quash all diversity, the concept of a canon—a group of recognized authoritative texts—not only preceded the production of the New Testament but also led to the production of the books recognized as Scripture.[32] The concept of "canon" was a natural, early, and inevitable development in a movement with Jewish roots. The Jewish Scriptures were built around the concept of a covenant that issued in written texts. With this background, combined with the belief that God had finally instituted the new covenant foretold by the prophets of old, the earliest Christians expected God also to supply written documents to accompany his new covenant as he did in the case of the old.[33]

---

[32] Ehrman refers to the canon as a "weapon" of the proto-orthodox in *Jesus, Interrupted*, 216.

[33] For a full treatment of this point, see Michal J. Kruger, *The Question of Canon* (Downers Grove: InterVarsity, 2013).

What is more, there is clear evidence from the New Testament itself that the earliest Christians had a theological category for "canon" and an understanding that a canon on par with the Old Testament canon was emerging. This list provides key examples from the New Testament:

- 2 Peter 3:16: *He [Paul] speaks about these things in all his letters in which there are some matters that are hard to understand. The untaught and unstable twist them to their own destruction, as they also do with the rest of the Scriptures.* Peter asserts that Paul's letters are Scripture on par with the Old Testament. He mentions this almost in passing, expecting his readers to know what he is talking about. An implication from this is that since Peter also refers to himself as an "apostle," the same authority can be transferred to his letters. Some, including Ehrman, have argued that 2 Peter was forged by an early second-century writer. We will leave our response to this argument to a later chapter;[34] yet it bears mentioning that even if one accepts a later authorship for 2 Peter, this verse demonstrates that by the end of the first century Christians already had a clear conception of an emerging new canon.
- 1 Timothy 5:18: *For the Scripture says, Do not muzzle an ox while it is treading out the grain, and, the worker is worthy of his wages.* Paul cites Deuteronomy 25:4, an Old Testament passage, alongside Luke 10:7 (a New Testament book citing the words of Jesus) and refers to both as "Scripture." Again, some have argued that 1 Timothy was actually written by someone other than Paul around AD 100. We believe there are good reasons for accepting Paul's authorship of this letter in the 60s.[35] Yet even if one allows more skeptical scholars to use their date, this passage would still show that by the end of the first century Christians were already putting Luke's Gospel on par with the Old Testament Scriptures.

---

[34] See chapter 5.

[35] See *The Cradle, the Cross, and the Crown*, 639–42, and Donald Guthrie, *New Testament Introduction*, 2nd ed. (Downers Grove: InterVarsity, 1990), 607–49.

- 2 Peter 3:2: *That you can remember the words previously spoken of the holy prophets and the command of our Lord and Savior given through your apostles.* Here the written words of the Old Testament prophets are placed alongside the testimony of the New Testament apostles, implying that the latter, like the former, were viewed as divine revelation.

The Contents of the New Testament Canon

In the next chapter we will address in greater detail the question of why certain books mentioned by Ehrman in his arguments were not recognized as Scripture. At this point a few general comments concerning the claim that a canon was imposed onto the early church must suffice. The assumption made by Ehrman is that there was nothing to distinguish the New Testament documents from other writings.[36] By listing various heretical writings, Ehrman makes it appear that the process by which books made it into the canon was somewhat of a free-for-all. However, listing books completed in the mid to late second and third centuries makes little difference in a discussion concerned with the New Testament since all the books included in the canon were completed by around AD 100 at the latest.

Moreover, as will become evident in the next chapter, the historical credentials of the books listed by Ehrman do not compare to those of the New Testament documents. For example, the Gospels written by Matthew, Mark, Luke, and John are first-century documents; the *Gospel of Thomas*, for example, dates to the second century. What is more, the *Gospel of Thomas* is not a Gospel; that is, it does not contain a continual narrative of the life, death, and resurrection of the Lord Jesus Christ. Also, Ehrman illegitimately excludes the notion of the Holy Spirit as God's means of guiding early Christians to recognize God-inspired Scripture. Those who believe in a personal God, on the other hand, should have no problems accepting the possibility that God was at work through his

---

[36] This contrasts with the view of Ehrman's teacher at Princeton, Bruce Metzger, who explicitly argues that these books showed themselves to be authoritative by their wide early use. See Metzger, *The Canon of the New Testament: Its Origin, Development, and Significance* (Oxford: Clarendon, 1987), 282–88.

Spirit to guide the formation of the New Testament canon.[37] But even as a historical matter for those who question any explicit theological criteria, the vast majority of books that made it into the New Testament had come to have a reputation for being valuable before any authoritative collection was named by any council. Irenaeus names more than twenty of these books at the end of the second century, long before any church councils of the fourth and fifth centuries.

Preaching to the Choir

As Ehrman closes his book *Lost Christianities*, he ties his grand narrative of early diversity to some pastoral implications:

> The broader interest in and heightened apprecia-
> tion for diverse manifestations of religious experi-
> ence, belief, and practice today has contributed to a
> greater fascination with the diverse expressions of
> Christianity in various periods of its history, per-
> haps especially in its earliest period. This fascina-
> tion is not simply a matter of antiquarian interest.
> There is instead a sense that alternative under-
> standings of Christianity from the past can be
> cherished yet today, that they can provide insights
> even now for those of us who are concerned about
> the world and our place in it. Those captivated
> with this fascination commonly feel a sense of loss
> upon realizing just how many perspectives once
> endorsed by well-meaning, intelligent, and sincere

---

[37] See Michael J. Kruger, *Canon Revisited: Establishing the Origins and Authority of the New Testament Books* (Wheaton: Crossway, 2012). Kruger makes the epistemological point that once one appeals to an external source to authorize a source one is seeking to prove authoritative, the external source becomes the authority. For instance, if one turns to one's own historical research as the authoritative guide for determining what is canonical, then the question still remains: What authorizes the authority of one's historical reasoning? Consequently, Kruger argues that for the canon to be the canon, it must in certain ways be self-authenticating. He does not deny that external historical information has an important place in determining the canon but contends that the core component for determining the canonical writings is "the internal marks of their divinity" (p. 90). Kruger proposes that with regard to canon, "the Scriptures themselves provide the grounds for considering external data: the apostolicity of books, the testimony of the church, and so forth" (ibid.).

believers came to be abandoned, destroyed, and forgotten—as were the texts that these believers produced, read, and revered.[38]

Although Ehrman claims to have given up his days of preaching, this is an example of sermonizing at its finest. A good preacher, no matter the validity of the theology behind his message, understands how to handle the details of the texts and weave them into a larger narrative that moves his listeners. A well-trained preacher refuses to stop at having the congregation adhere to abstract beliefs but seeks to connect the belief system to current society and to direct people how to live. Ehrman, in better form than many contemporary preachers, has connected his grand narrative of the early church to modern-day application, with the invitation to cherish "alternative forms of Christianity." Despite Ehrman's rhetorical flourishes, however, he ultimately fails to carry out the role of objective historian. His "sermon," which celebrates diversity, is well received as he preaches to the choir of postmodern culture. Yet if Ehrman's listeners are willing to "uncover their ears" to hear, they will find that the historical evidence for Ehrman's own grand narrative is simply not there.

Discussion Questions

1. Explain Walter Bauer's view on early Christianity.
2. What are some of the problems with Bauer's thesis?
3. How did the early church distinguish heresy from orthodoxy?
4. What biblical evidence suggests that the church viewed many of the New Testament books as Scripture upon, or soon after, receiving them?
5. What is the evidence in favor of the early church having a built-in expectation for a New Testament canon?

---

[38] Ehrman, *Lost Christianities*, 257.

Chapter Five

ARE MANY NEW TESTAMENT DOCUMENTS FORGED?

Claims Addressed
---

1. The New Testament Gospels are not historically reliable and are comparable to the various other "heretical" gospels because they were not actually written by Jesus' companions.

2. The first disciples were illiterate and therefore could not have written the parts of the New Testament attributed to them.

3. Many of the New Testament books were not really written by the authors to whom they were ascribed, despite the internal claims of the books themselves. Instead, they were forged.

4. Other forms of Christianity are represented in various other writings, which have equally as valid a claim to Christianity as the twenty-seven canonical New Testament books.

5. The "proto-orthodox" used the canon as a weapon to impose their own brand of theology on all forms of Christianity and eventually succeeded in the fourth century by way of the powerful church of this period.

Forgery and Bringing the New Testament Down

Imagine 2,000 years from now someone visiting a library containing some ancient writings. He happens to stumble upon an entire section of books from the first part of the twenty-first century, all bearing the name of Bart Ehrman. The man's interest is sparked by the antiquity of the collection and the books' curious titles. As he reads through the extant collection of Ehrman's writings, he comes across some quotes that seem to be in tension. For instance, he reads a passage Ehrman wrote in 2009:

> And so we have an answer to our ultimate question of why these Gospels are so different from one another. They were not written by Jesus' companion or by companions. They were written decades later by people who didn't know Jesus, who lived in a different country or different countries from Jesus. They are different from each other in part because they also didn't know each other, to some extent they had different sources of information (although Matthew and Luke drew on Mark), and they modified their stories on the basis of their own understanding of who Jesus was.[1]

Ehrman paints a fairly hopeless picture: the New Testament Gospels were written by people who lived long after Jesus, had no way of knowing if what they were recording was historical, and felt free to modify the traditions based on their own understanding (even though they didn't know what actually happened, only what their sources told them). On the other hand, the same library visitor reads in another book by Ehrman, published in 2011, just a couple of years after the previous quote,

> [I]f historians want to know what Jesus said and did they are more or less constrained to use the New Testament Gospels as their principal sources. Let me emphasize that this is not for religious or theological reasons—for instance, that these and these alone can be trusted. It is for historical reasons, pure and simple. . . . Moreover, the Gospel accounts outside the New Testament tend to be

---

[1] Bart D. Ehrman, *Jesus, Interrupted: Revealing the Hidden Contradictions in the Bible (And Why We Don't Know about Them)* (San Francisco: HarperOne, 2009), 112.

> late and legendary, of considerable interest in
> and of themselves, but of little use to the histo-
> rian interested in knowing what happened during
> Jesus' lifetime. . . . [T]he only real sources avail-
> able to the historian interested in the life of Jesus
> are therefore the New Testament Gospels.[2]

What should the man of the future conclude from these two different statements from Ehrman? He could imagine the author changed his position along the way. Or he could presume that the author's position developed in a way that was not contradictory to his initial position. Or he could assume he had yet to grasp fully Ehrman's position—perhaps due to the historical and cultural distance from the author or failure to integrate correctly all of his statements. Or the reader could simply assume one of the books was forged. These are just some of the possibilities that would explain these two statements. The correct explanation for apparent tension is not the point. The point is that plenty of options account for tension. Forgery is one possibility, but, assuming publishers would not have wanted to sign off on something Ehrman had not actually written, it seems rather remote. Only unwarranted cynicism would cause the person to conclude that one of the books said to be written by Ehrman was actually forged.

Though this is a hypothetical situation and the analogy is not perfect, both of the above statements are actually by Ehrman (or at least we assume they are). However, if the pattern Ehrman has set in evaluating New Testament authorship (see claim 3) were adopted, the reader would wrongly conclude that choosing any option other than forgery is nothing but a biased attempt to reconcile two contradictory statements and thus infer that Ehrman didn't really write one or both of the books. Of course, on the assumption that Ehrman did write both works, this conclusion would be wrong.

As mentioned, no analogy is perfect. Ehrman correctly points out that forgery was more common in the first century than it is

---

[2] Bart D. Ehrman, *The New Testament: A Historical Introduction to the Early Christian Writings*, 4th ed. (New York: Oxford University Press, 2011), 215.

in the twenty-first. Nevertheless, the example illustrates Ehrman's unwarranted skepticism, which consistently causes him to cry "Forgery!" when other more likely explanations are available. The evidence indicates that the early church was careful about what it included in the canon and was particularly on the lookout for forgeries. They did not want to endorse a forgery any more than a modern-day publisher would want to sign off on a book that is counterfeit. Generally, the tendency was for the early church to reject rather than accept books whose authorship was in question.[3] In view of this caution by the early church, and in contrast to Ehrman, New Testament scholar Mike Licona sets forth a more suitable approach:

> Before jettisoning belief in the traditional author-ship of any of the 27, the arguments against it must be reasonably stronger than the arguments for it and be able to withstand the counterargu-ments. Some like Ehrman appear to take a dif-ferent approach, assuming that all of the 27 are guilty of false attribution until nearly unimpeach-able evidence to the contrary can be presented. Evidence of this approach can be seen when the evidence for traditional authorship is dismissed too quickly or when arguments against the tradi-tional authorship are strikingly weak.[4]

Ehrman's argument that much of the New Testament was forged is part of his larger overall narrative where the canon of the New Testament is recast as a historical accident that could have easily featured some not so orthodox (i.e., apocryphal) writings. In order to make such a case, he must demonstrate that Christian heretical writings of the second and third centuries rival the his-torical credentials of the New Testament documents. However, Ehrman is too good a scholar to argue that these heretical writings

---

[3] The New Testament book of Hebrews is the exception that proves the rule.

[4] Michael Licona, "Review of *Forged: Writing in the Name of God—Why the Bible's Authors Are Not Who We Think They Are*," 2–3. Accessed June 21, 2012 http://www.risenjesus.com/articles/52-review-of-forged.

have historical merit. Therefore, instead of attempting to bring the apocryphal writings *up* by arguing for their historical credentials, he brings the New Testament documents *down*, attempting to make their historical merits (or demerits) resemble these other writings. Thus, according to Ehrman, Jesus' disciples were illiterate backwoods peasants; the New Testament writings were not written by Jesus' disciples or their associates; much of the New Testament was forged; and even if the New Testament were based on eyewitness testimony, it cannot be trusted because even eyewitnesses are biased.

In order to respond to these kinds of claims, this chapter has been divided into five portions. The first three arguments respond to various reasons given by Ehrman, who contends that the New Testament lacks historical credentials and therefore cannot be trusted. (1) The Gospels were not written by the first disciples or their associates, in particular because (2) the disciples were illiterate and (3) much of the New Testament was forged. The response to claim 4 provides a survey of second- and third-century (and even later) writings that Ehrman presents as virtually indistinguishable from the New Testament documents. The evidence demonstrates that these later works do not contain anything close to the historical merits of the books of the New Testament. Finally, in the response to claim 5, the canon turns out to be the expression of the first-century belief that God has spoken through Jesus Christ as the fulfillment of the Old Testament promises of a Messiah.

The New Testament Documents: Real or Counterfeit?

Claim 1:   *The New Testament Gospels are not historically reliable and are comparable to the various other "heretical" gospels because they were not actually written by Jesus' companions.*

Much of Ehrman's skepticism toward the New Testament Gospels is bound up in his distrust for the Gospel authors themselves. He argues the tradition concerning their authorship arose in order to assure readers that they were written by eyewitnesses and associates of eyewitnesses. Ehrman argues that even if the Gospels were based on eyewitness testimony, due to their biases "the reality is that eyewitnesses cannot be trusted to give historically accurate accounts."[5]

Ehrman's argument has several problems. First, he fails to explain why, if the church wanted to use early church figures to gain widespread acceptance for these documents, they chose Matthew, Mark, and Luke, three rather obscure figures in early Christianity. If all the early church did was assign names to the Gospel documents in order to invest them with greater authority, it seems they would have chosen authors who occupied more significant roles among Jesus' inner circle.

This point can be illustrated rather vividly using Mark's Gospel as the example. In the Ehrman model, one picks an author to enhance the stature of a work whose real author is unknown. So you can pick anyone to fill in the knowledge gap. In the case of Mark, early in the church Mark was understood to be the author who drew on Peter's preaching. Now let's consider Mark's credentials according to Acts. (1) He failed to make it successfully through the first missionary journey and went home to Mama. (2) He caused a rift between Paul and Barnabas before the second missionary journey. These are hardly credentials to enhance a work's credibility. On the other side is Peter, a well-known and highly regarded early apostle. Now you have a choice to select between Mark and Peter an author to enhance the credibility of the work. Whom would you choose? Peter is the natural choice. He has far more credentials to enhance the work. Yet the tradition selects Mark. The tradition must know something to make this choice. The alternative model cannot really explain it.

Second, it is wrong to suppose that a person with a vested interest is necessarily an unreliable witness. Greek and Roman historians believed ideal eyewitnesses were participants in an event who were able to draw on their experience to interpret its significance rather than dispassionate observers.[6] Ehrman is correct to argue that eyewitnesses don't always necessarily get things

---

[5] Ehrman, *Jesus, Interrupted*, 103.
[6] Samuel Byrskog, *Story as History—History as Story: The Gospel Tradition in the Context of*

completely right. But if the Gospels are based on eyewitness testimony, it seems sensible to assume that eyewitnesses were passionate about making sure the events surrounding the life of Jesus were reported accurately.[7]

Finally, Ehrman fails to grapple with important contributions in recent scholarship which significantly challenge the belief that the Gospels were not based on eyewitness testimony. For the first 1,800 years of Christian history, the predominant view was that the New Testament Gospels were reliable documents derived from eyewitness testimony. To access the Jesus of history was to go to the Jesus of the four canonical Gospels. However, Ehrman is among the many critical scholars who now believe the Gospels were not based on eyewitness accounts. Yet this negative stance toward the Gospels' reliability is increasingly being challenged.

Richard Bauckham's *Jesus and the Eyewitnesses*, in particular, has set forth substantial evidence that the canonical Gospels are based on eyewitness testimony and thus can be trusted.[8] Bauckham argues that a group of scholars in the early twentieth century (called "form critics") got modern scholarship off track. Central in their approach was the belief that the Gospels were akin to folk literature, similar to old German fairy tales, the product of oral traditions passed down by people who had no interest in history. Similarly, stories about Jesus were passed down orally by way of anonymous community traditions in the early church. Rather than showing interest in history, these people felt free to modify traditions to meet the current needs of their community.[9] Most

---

Ancient Oral History, Wissenschaftliche Untersuchungen zum Neuen Testament 123 (Tübingen: Mohr-Siebeck, 2000), 64.

[7] See claim 4 in chapter 4. Important here is work by Robert K. McIver, *Memory, Jesus and the Synoptic Gospels*, Resources for Biblical Study 59 (Atlanta: Society of Biblical Literature, 2011). He surveys studies on memory and argues that the case for retaining the core of an event in such cases is strong. I (Bock) once debated with John Dominic Crossan about memory. He cited a famous Emory University study of students and the *Challenger* disaster to argue for how fickle memory is. I countered by asking if the results might have been different if astronauts had been surveyed instead since they had a stake in riding such a spacecraft and there would be corporate memory at work as well. The church had a stake in their memory commitments to Jesus because of persecution and the threat of martyrdom. Such factors need to be recalled in these debates over memory.

[8] Richard Bauckham, *Jesus and the Eyewitnesses: The Gospels as Eyewitness Testimony* (Grand Rapids: Eerdmans, 2006).

[9] For a response to the form critics' assumption that the Gospels were written for isolated,

scholars agree that Jesus' disciples and other eyewitnesses to his ministry communicated the original Gospel traditions. However, these critics assumed the eyewitnesses disappeared from the scene, which allowed for the original traditions to be altered with little concern for history during the above-described anonymous transmission process in the early church. Ehrman basically seems to accept this model.[10]

However, Bauckham's building on the work of others has severely crippled this form-critical model.[11] He argues that the standard form-critical picture is highly unlikely since many of the eyewitnesses were alive and active in the early church until well after the Gospels were written. These eyewitnesses would have functioned as authoritative sources or guardians of the tradition, which was common in oral societies. The following is a brief survey of Bauckham's argument.

First, Bauckham shows that in ancient Mediterranean times, historians relied as much as they could on eyewitness testimony.[12] The opening four verses of Luke match established language used by historians of the day and show the care taken in the composition of the Gospel. Moreover, in ancient history, just as in all of history, eyewitness testimony was, by its nature, selective. The Gospels provide four different perspectives because they are from four different authors who experienced events differently or utilized their sources differently.

Second, while Ehrman quickly dismisses Papias—a pastor in the second century from whom we have testimony—as unreliable and irrelevant to the discussion of authorship, Bauckham traces

specific communities see Richard Bauckham, ed., *The Gospels for All Christians: Rethinking the Gospel Audiences* (Grand Rapids: Eerdmans, 1998).

[10] Bart D. Ehrman, *Did Jesus Exist? The Historical Argument for Jesus of Nazareth* (San Francisco: HarperOne, 2012), 83–85.

[11] Birger Gerhardsson, *The Reliability of Gospel Tradition* (Peabody, MA: Hendrickson, 2001); idem, *Memory and Manuscript with Tradition and Transmission in Early Christianity* (Grand Rapids: Eerdmans, 1998); Byrskog, *Story as History—History as Story*. Especially important is the work by Ken Bailey, who lived in an oral culture and has challenged the form-critical model by arguing for a form of orality that is controlled but informal in its approach. He notes how a corporate culture keeps a solid hand on the gist of accounts that are passed on orally. Kenneth E. Bailey, "Informal Controlled Oral Tradition and the Synoptic Gospels," *Themelios* 20, no. 2 (January 1995): 4–11.

[12] Bauckman, *Jesus and the Eyewitnesses*, 1–11, 116–24.

out the evidence for Papias's reliability and the implications of his writings.[13] Bauckham shows how Papias identifies three generations: (1) eyewitnesses, (2) the elders who sat at their feet, and (3) the disciples of the elders. Papias claims that when he was a young man (in the AD 80s at the latest), many members of these three generations were still alive, including the eyewitnesses. Most scholars affirm that by this time at least Mark's Gospel had been completed and Matthew and Luke were being written or had been completed as well. This evidence points to the Gospels not being merely based on oral traditions passed down and altered during the various stages of transmission but on oral history communicated by eyewitness testimony.

Third, Bauckham argues that the names present in the Gospels themselves are meant to assure the readers of their accuracy.[14] He shows how throughout the Gospels some figures are distinguished by use of their proper names while others are left nameless. He then describes the various theories proposed for this phenomenon and the weaknesses of each theory. He concludes that the names were meant to serve as living guarantors of the tradition. In particular, he notes the fascinating phenomenon that while typically the longer past a given event an account is written, the less specificity; we see in the Gospels the opposite scenario. John's Gospel, which almost certainly was the last of the four canonical Gospels written, records names of people in the gospel story such as Lazarus (whom Jesus raised from the dead) or Malchus (the high priest's servant whose ear Peter cut off at Jesus' arrest).

Why is it that contrary to what would be expected in the case of the transmission of community tradition, these names are not mentioned in the earlier Gospels (Matthew, Mark, Luke) but then suddenly pop up at a later point in time? Bauckham's answer: "protective anonymity," by which he means the practice of leaving the identity of a person concealed for protective purposes as long as he or she is still alive while revealing it once the person has died and is no longer the possible subject of persecution.[15] In other words,

---

[13] Ibid., 12–38, 202–39, 412–37.

[14] Ibid., 39–239.

[15] In this Bauckham draws on the work of scholar Gerd Theissen.

Matthew, or Mark and Luke, did not mention particular names as long as certain characters were still alive while John was free to reveal their identities because by his time these people had passed away. This shows how many characters in the gospel story were still living during the time the earlier Gospels were written.

Or take the "*inclusio* of eyewitness testimony" as another example, the identification of the primary witness on which a given Gospel is based at the beginning and the end of a given Gospel (e.g., Peter in Mark). Again, this shows the Gospel writers' conscious dependence on eyewitness testimony. John, for his part, has a pronounced "witness" motif (as does Luke in both of his volumes: the Gospel and the book of Acts). He asserts that John the Baptist served as a witness to Jesus (not merely as the one who baptized him at the beginning of his ministry), as did God the Father, the Holy Spirit, Jesus' own works, and John the evangelist himself.[16] In fact, John makes clear that he personally was present in the upper room at the Last Supper, at the events surrounding Jesus' arrest and trial, at the cross, at the empty tomb, and at Jesus' postresurrection appearances.[17] This greatly underscores the reliability of John's testimony in his Gospel.

Fourth, in response to those who claim primitive societies cannot distinguish between myth and history, Bauckham surveys work in the field of oral traditions in primitive African cultures.[18] His survey concludes that fictional and historical stories are clearly distinguishable and that primitive societies take much greater care to preserve historical accounts.

Finally, Bauckham explores studies in the field of psychology, specifically about the nature and reliability of memory.[19] Marks of eyewitness testimony in the Gospels include vividness, excess detail, vantage point, and perspective. These features stand in stark contrast to fictional accounts of the time.

Bauckham demonstrates there is good warrant for taking each of the four canonical Gospels as offering different perspectives on

---

[16] The Johannine "witness theme" spans all the way from John 1:6–8 to 21:24–25.

[17] See John 13:23; 18:15–16; 19:35; 20:2, 8; 21:2, 7–8.

[18] Bauckham, *Jesus and the Eyewitnesses*, 264–89; cf. Jan Vansina, *Oral Tradition as History* (Madison, WI: University of Wisconsin Press, 1985).

[19] Bauckham, *Jesus and the Eyewitnesses*, 290–357.

history. Once it is accepted that the Gospels were written based on eyewitness testimony, the burden of proof lies on the *critic* to demonstrate that the accounts are *not* historically plausible rather than on the *Gospels* to prove their reliability.

Other than by quick dismissal of Papias, Ehrman never engages or even footnotes these types of arguments made by scholars concerning the eyewitness testimony of the Gospels in any of his popular works. Has he not read Bauckham's seminal work published in 2006? Is he unaware of its existence? This lack of engagement with opposing views in Ehrman's works can result in a kind of academic bullying: lay readers are backed into a corner with nowhere to turn because, according to Ehrman, all good scholarship agrees with him. The average person, unaware of scholars who see things differently from Ehrman, can easily feel there are only two options: agree with Ehrman that what he falsely implies is basically the opinion of the rest of biblical scholarship or shut his or her eyes and hum to avoid hearing the evidence (in keeping with Ehrman's own caricature). However, *Jesus and the Eyewitnesses* is just one example among many that proves Ehrman is not giving the complete picture of what some of the best contemporary scholarship (not necessarily evangelical) is saying.[20]

Claim 2: *The first disciples were illiterate and therefore could not have written the parts of the New Testament attributed to them.*

Literacy and education were of concern to first-century Jews and were promoted for boys starting from the age of six or seven.[21] Sociologists tell us that ethnic identity among minorities

---

[20] See, for example, Ehrman's work *Jesus, Interrupted*, which does not include a single reference to Bauckham's work. *Jesus, Interrupted* was published in 2009 while Bauckham's work appeared in 2006. Thus, it would seem reasonable to expect Ehrman to incorporate scholarly interaction with Bauckham in his subsequent work.

[21] The often-cited work on literacy in the larger Greco-Roman world, William V. Harris, *Ancient Literacy* (Cambridge, MA: Harvard University Press, 1989), estimates literacy rates to be somewhere between 10 and 15 percent. Others have suggested an even smaller percentage of literacy among those in the Greco-Roman culture. But, would first-century Judaism necessarily have the same literacy rates as the broader culture? In two interesting articles—Maristella Botticini and Zvi Eckstein, "From Farmers to Merchants, Voluntary Conversions and Diaspora: A Human Capital Interpretation of Jewish History," *Journal of the European Economic Association* 55 (2007) and Maristella Botticini and Zvi Eckstein, "Jewish Occupational Selection: Education,

leads them to pursue careful passing on of ethnic traditions to preserve their way of life. Also, archaeological discoveries in Galilee
demonstrate there was more of a concern with following Jewish
practice and legal awareness than was once thought. This assumes
a more literate culture, at least on an oral level.

Ben Witherington responds pointedly to Ehrman's specific
argument that the first disciples were mere illiterate peasants:

> First of all, fishermen are not peasants. They often
> made a good living from the Sea of Galilee, as can
> be seen from the famous and large fisherman's
> house excavated in Bethsaida. Secondly, fisher-
> men were businessmen and they had to either
> have a scribe or be able to read and write a bit to
> deal with tax collectors, toll collectors, and other
> business persons. Thirdly, if indeed Jesus had a
> Matthew/Levi and others who were tax collectors
> as disciples, they were indeed literate, and again
> were not peasants. As the story of Zacchaeus
> makes perfectly clear, they could indeed have
> considerable wealth, sometimes from bilking
> people out of their money. In other words, it is a
> caricature to suggest that all Jesus' disciples were
> illiterate peasants.[22]

Restrictions, or Minorities," *Journal of Economic History* 65, no. 4 (2005)—these economists
trace the Jewish success in urban occupations in later history back to the enforced religious
norms of Jewish fathers educating their children beginning in the second century BC. Although
they suggest these norms did not increase the literacy rate among Jews until later (around the
end of the second century AD), we would submit it is more likely that these norms had an
impact on literacy among Jews by the first century AD: see Craig A. Evans, "Context, Family,
and Formation," in *The Cambridge Companion to Jesus*, Cambridge Companions to Religion, ed.
Markus Bockmuehl (Cambridge: Cambridge University Press, 2001), 11–24; Paul Foster, "Educating Jesus: The Search for a Plausible Context," *JSHJ* 4 (2006): 7–33; and for a magisterial study
of Jewish education in first-century Palestine, see Rainer Riesner, *Jesus als Lehrer: Eine Unter-
suchung zum Ursprung der Evangelien-Überlieferung*, Wissenschaftliche Untersuchungen zum
Neuen Testament 2/7, 3rd ed. (Tübingen: Mohr-Siebeck, 1988). Unfortunately, this study has yet
to be translated into English. Also see Alan Millard, *Reading and Writing in the Time of Jesus*,
The Biblical Seminar 69 (Sheffield, UK: Sheffield Academic Press, 2000), who argues not only
that literacy rates among Jewish males in particular were higher but that the literacy rates among
that more general Greco-Roman culture were higher than suggested by William V. Harris.
[22] Ben Witherington III, "Bart Interrupted," http://benwitherington.blogspot.com/2009/04.

In particular, Ehrman uses Peter as an example of "a back-woods illiterate peasant" who would not have been literate enough to write the Gospels.[23] Therefore, Peter serves as a test case for the problems in Ehrman's larger argument concerning the disciples' illiteracy.

Ehrman has ignored certain things we know about Peter and his context. Apparently, Peter was literate enough to lead and help launch a religious movement that spanned continents by the time of his death. Peter led this movement in Greco-Roman contexts outside of Israel, as well as in the land. In the Greco-Roman settings, Greek would have been the main language. This means he must have been a solid oral communicator at the least, making him potentially capable of expressing himself in letters. Some of this communication took place in a context where Greek would have been important. In an *oral* culture he need only be able to *dictate* in order to compose his letters. Ehrman's argument seems trapped in a *literary* model of communication, not the predominantly oral world of the first century. Even if Ehrman were right about literacy and Peter (a point we are about to challenge), his conclusion regarding Peter's linguistic ability does not hold in an oral context.

The argument for Peter's illiteracy can also be challenged in light of Peter's role as a merchant tradesman and what was likely the case with education in the first century among Jews. Evidence exists of extensive commerce and knowledge of Greek in Tiberias and Sepphoris, both of which are located close to Capernaum and Nazareth respectively. In fact, these larger Sea of Galilee communities are seen as so important that John Dominic Crossan, hardly a conservative interpreter of Scripture, argues that Jesus would almost certainly have practiced carpentry in Sepphoris and engaged in a kind of international trade and exchange of ideas. All of this assumes some level of linguistic and cultural engagement.

Ehrman's argument that Peter and John were illiterate based on translating *agrammatoi* in Acts 4:13 as "illiterate" completely misses the point. The word *agrammatoi* is the opposite of

---

[23] Bart D. Ehrman, *Forged: Writing in the Name of God—Why the Bible's Authors Are Not Who We Think They Are* (San Francisco, HarperOne, 2011), 75.

grammatoi, which commonly in New Testament times denoted formal education if not professional scribal training. Therefore, *agrammatoi* can simply mean a person lacked formal or rabbinic schooling.[24] What is more, in the context of Acts 4, it is not the case that the authorities were surprised because they thought Peter and John were *knowledgeable* when in fact they were *ignorant*. The opposite is true: the authorities were surprised because they thought they would be *ignorant* and instead they proved to be *knowledgeable*. Moreover, as mentioned, many Jewish boys did learn to read, and since John's family was not poor (Luke 5:3 and Mark 1:20 indicate that his family owned boats and employed others), it is highly probable that he received a better-than-average education.[25]

Nothing discussed up to this point even considers the possible presence of amanuenses or secretaries who might have helped New Testament authors put oral Greek into written forms of communication if such help was needed.[26] The point is simply that everything we know about the scope of Peter's ministry outside Israel points to someone with exposure to and some facility in Greek.

That said, there is a high probability that the New Testament authors, such as Paul, did in fact use secretaries; it is certainly possible that Peter did as well. Even Ehrman admits, "Virtually all of the problems with what I've been calling forgeries can be solved if secretaries were heavily involved in the composition of the early Christian writings."[27] However, strangely, Ehrman argues that secretaries only involved themselves in these works in exceptional cases and for the upper class. But how does Ehrman know this?

---

[24] See Craig Evans, "Jewish Scripture and the Literacy of Jesus," accessed 10 October 2013 at http://www.craigaevans.com/evans.pdf.

[25] D. A. Carson goes further, adding, "Rabbi Akiba was apparently unlettered until the age of forty, and then became one of the greatest rabbis of his generation; it would not be surprising if some of the leaders of the church, decades after its founding, had devoted themselves to some serious study" (*The Gospel According to John*, Pillar New Testament Commentary [Grand Rapids: Eerdmans, 1991], 74).

[26] Here the work of E. Randolph Richards is important in two key works, *Paul and First Century Letter Writing: Secretaries, Composition and Collection* (Downers Grove: InterVarsity, 2004); and *The Secretaries in the Letters of Paul* (Wissenschaftliche Untersuchungen zum Neuen Testament 2/42; Tübingen: Mohr-Siebeck, 1991). He argues that the use of secretaries allows writers to dictate their materials, and the secretary will help with the composition. His study interacts with the ancient literature on this practice.

[27] Ehrman, *Forged*, 134.

The reason he connects the practice to the upper class is because the literature we have that relates these texts comes from the upper classes. But if a secretary does this for people with more education, why would he not do so for those with less education, people who would be less likely to be able to write for themselves? Not only is there good evidence that the early disciples, such as Peter, were able communicators, but there is also no reason to assume they wrote their letters without the help of secretaries.

Claim 3: *Many of the New Testament books were not really written by the authors to whom they were ascribed, despite the internal claims of the books themselves. Instead, they were forged.*

In his book *Forged*, Ehrman has cast aspersions on the traditional authorship of the biblical materials by presenting examples of how often forgery was committed in the second and third centuries in books that were not in the New Testament canon. In order to put the New Testament books in the same category as these later forgeries, Ehrman dismisses external tradition, contradicts his own arguments, minimizes the influence of secretaries, and constructs a portrait of conflict and diversity in the early church that the early sources do not support. This list of dubious moves is so long and Ehrman makes them so effortlessly that it is easy to see why an unsuspecting reader might think Ehrman has made a good case.

Pointing out all the glitches in each of Ehrman's supporting points for forgery is beyond the scope of this chapter. The following four responses to Ehrman's arguments will address test cases that have wider implications since these types of claims lodged by Ehrman for forgery in certain New Testament books occur frequently in his writings.

Test Case 1: *First Peter was forged (1) because it is in error concerning the author's claim that Peter witnessed Jesus' suffering and (2) because of its use of*

"Babylon" as a code word for Rome,
which reflects post-AD 70 usage.

The first argument fails because it defines the suffering of Jesus as the crucifixion. Only this is too narrow. In fact, the available evidence doesn't make clear whether Peter watched the events of the crucifixion from afar, as did the Galilean women, or not. Yet unlike others, Peter did not flee when Jesus was arrested but saw the arrest and followed him to his Jewish examination to watch from a distance (even though with the timidity of denying him three times).[28] This detail about the denials makes it unlikely that this story was made up, as it is an embarrassment for Peter. Most plausibly, therefore, Peter did witness some of the suffering and mocking of Jesus, even if (for argument's sake) he may not have observed the crucifixion itself.

The second argument, likewise, is not as persuasive as it might seem. There is ample biblical and extrabiblical ancient precedent for a world power being named by the use of code language (see, e.g., the book of Daniel and the way it pictures the world's kingdoms in an end-time vision). Among other reasons, this was done for "in-house purposes" to veil the identity of an opposing nation in order to minimize persecution. It also linked opposing world powers in the history of God's people to form a chain of evil nations, whether Egypt (the exodus), Assyria and Babylon (the exile), or Rome (the prevailing world power at the time of Jesus' ministry and the emergence of the early church). What all these nations shared in common was opposition to Yahweh, the one true God, and the practice of idolatry and polytheism, the worship of multiple gods.

Rome, the latest incarnation of such evil opposition to the worship of God on a national scale, engaged in emperor worship and turned increasingly hostile toward believers in Jesus, culminating in the fire of Rome (AD 64) which Nero blamed on the Christians and which resulted in major persecutions under emperors Nero (AD 54–68) and Domitian (AD 81–96).[29] By call-

---

[28] See, e.g., Matthew 26 and parallels.

[29] On the emperor cult, see Köstenberger, Kellum, and Quarles, *The Cradle, the Cross, and*

ing Rome "Babylon," therefore, an identification was made that linked present-day Rome to previous opposition to God's people by the Babylonians and other nations. What is more, such code language to describe the opponents of God's people was not limited to Scripture. The Dead Sea community, for instance, which did not survive beyond the fall of Jerusalem and the destruction of the temple in AD 70, used similar terminology, calling the Romans "Kittim." As for the respect for government evident in Peter's first epistle, Christians, as a politically and socioeconomically powerless minority, had to take care when addressing Rome. For these and other reasons, this argument, too, is problematic and fails to persuade.

Test Case 2: *Second Peter was forged because (1) the notion of a delay in Jesus' return fits a later, rather than earlier, setting; (2) the author makes use of the book of Jude; and (3) Paul did not claim to write Scripture, so the notion of an authoritative collection of Pauline letters on par with the Old Testament belongs to a later period.*

First, is it true that the notion of a delay in Jesus' return belongs exclusively to the later New Testament period? In fact, the evidence points to the contrary. First Thessalonians, which most scholars accept as having been written by Paul in the early AD 50s, shows a church anxious about issues surrounding Jesus' return. There were questions as to whether the event had already happened or had been delayed, and believers were urged to hold onto their faith diligently until the Second Coming. This makes clear that already the church was grappling with the apparent delay of Jesus' return in the period preceding the year 70 when the Jewish temple was destroyed. It is therefore illegitimate to cite the discussion of a delay in Jesus' return in 2 Peter as evidence for late authorship.

Second, the tradition about how Mark was connected with Peter with regard to the second Gospel may be relevant here.

---

the Crown: An Introduction to the New Testament (Nashville: B&H Academic, 2009), chap. 20, esp. 815–22.

According to the witness of some of the second-century church leaders, Peter's preaching informed Mark's Gospel, even though the church never called the Second Gospel (Mark) the Gospel *of Peter*.[30] If this Markan association is correct (which is likely), we see that Peter was not averse to associate his ministry with the name and work of another. If so, his possible use of Jude (if Jude indeed was written first) likewise would not be a problem. To the contrary, Peter's use of some of Jude's material shows the unity of the biblical writers, indicating that Peter was not above drawing on the teaching of others if it advanced the cause of the gospel in a given situation.

Third, Paul insisted on his authority as an apostle from the moment he wrote his New Testament letters. One only has to look at the tone of Galatians (written in the late 40s or early 50s) or the direct claims in 1 Thessalonians and 1 and 2 Corinthians. For instance, in 1 Thessalonians 4:15 Paul writes, "For we say this to you by a revelation from the Lord." In 1 Corinthians 2:13 Paul asserts, "We also speak these things, not in words taught by human wisdom, but in those taught by the Spirit, explaining spiritual things to spiritual people"; and later in the same letter he says, "If anyone thinks he is a prophet or spiritual, he should recognize that what I write to you is the Lord's command" (14:37). All of these letters circulated among the churches early.

True, Paul did not say, "I am writing Scripture," but he did say that disagreeing with him about the gospel was grounds for being subject to anathema (a strong rebuke). Not only that, but even if an angel were to proclaim another gospel, it must be rejected. Paul's words sound like they were penned by someone confident he was proclaiming the Word of God. One need not have the exact *wording* of Paul saying, "I am writing Scripture" for the *concept* to be present. So, at least for those churches that accepted Paul, these letters would have borne considerable authority right from the start.

Finally, if 2 Peter was a forgery by an unknown author, what would have been that author's motive? In the unambiguous examples of heretical forgeries, there appears to be some kind of

---

[30] We discussed this tradition earlier. These references can be found in Irenaeus, *Against Heresies* 3.1.1 and Eusebius, *Ecclesiastical History* 3.39.15–16.

subversive agenda. For example, the forged *Gospel of Peter* was written to promote a denial of the humanity of Christ.[31] But why would the orthodox need to use this type of device if "their teaching was consistent with the church already and thus they would have no motive to promote it falsely under the name of an apostle?"[32] In the case of 2 Peter, there seems no convincing reason why the orthodox would need to forge this letter and slip it into the canon since "it has no evident heterodoxical agenda, bears no clear resemblance to any other pseudo-Petrine literature [i.e., literature that falsely claimed Peter as the author], and exhibits no references to any of the second-century doctrinal controversies."[33] In view of the evidence presented, 2 Peter was likely included in the canon for a simple but less scandalous reason: Peter actually wrote it.

Test Case 3: *Second Thessalonians cannot be by the same writer as 1 Thessalonians because 1 Thessalonians defends an intense belief in the imminence of Jesus' return while 2 Thessalonians argues that certain things must happen first.*

Second Thessalonians points to events associated with Jesus' return, events that precede this return, and events that indicate the return has not yet come (as some are arguing; see 2 Thess 2:1–2). In particular, we can anticipate an intense political uprising and emergence of the Antichrist. However, there is no indication that such events preclude an imminent return of Jesus following them. In fact, the impression is that the return comes on the heels of events that trigger that return in such a way that these intervening events do not supply a long interruption or roadblock to the return but simply accompany it as it approaches quickly. The absence of these accompanying events simply means that the Day of the Lord has not yet come but says nothing about how close it is. Ehrman exaggerates the difference here.

---

[31] Docetism was a form of the Gnostic heresy, arguing that Jesus only *appeared* to be human (from the Greek word *dokeō*, "to seem").

[32] Michael J. Kruger, "The Authenticity of 2 Peter," *Journal of the Evangelical Theological Society* 42 (1999): 670.

[33] Ibid.

The tension between "soon" and "not so soon because other things will occur first" is not only found in Paul but also built into the understanding of the last days in the early church at large. For example, compare Matthew 24:33 ("when you see all these things, he is near") with 24:44b ("you also must be ready; because the Son of Man is coming at an hour you do not expect"). Luke 21:9 speaks of signs of pressure on Jerusalem but says the end "won't come right away." Yet the same author can declare in Luke 18:8 that the vindication of departed believers will come soon and in the same breath note that when the return comes, the delay will be long enough that the question can be raised, "Will the Son of Man find faith when he returns?"[34]

Similarly, 1 and 2 Thessalonians deal with the opposite elements in this inherent tension in Paul's end-time teaching. The swing this represents for the Thessalonians may only suggest that the reaction to Paul's initial letter became an overreaction in the other direction that also needed to be corrected. First Thessalonians says the people in that church hadn't missed the day yet—neither had those who had already died. Jesus' return was still coming anytime, possibly even soon. Second Thessalonians adds that these believers should not think the day has come yet, even though there are signs of judgment all around. Both of these teachings live in the tension of what the early church and Jesus taught; the end could come at any time but would ensue alongside major spiritual deterioration and desecration.

Test Case 4: *Paul did not write Ephesians because the style (mainly sentence length), vocabulary, and theology are distinct from his other letters.*

Ehrman argues that Ephesians' use of 116 words not present elsewhere in Paul shows its likely authorship by someone other than Paul. He goes on to note that this amount of unique vocabulary is 50 percent more than Philippians, which he claims is about the same length as Ephesians. Yet a closer look reveals that this

---

[34] See the discussion of this passage in Darrell L. Bock, *A Theology of Luke-Acts*, Biblical Theology of the New Testament (Grand Rapids: Zondervan, 2012), 399–400.

is inaccurate. Philippians has 104 verses, while Ephesians has 155 verses (in terms of Greek words, the ratio is 1,629 to 2,422 words). Ephesians is 33 percent longer than Philippians. Once this mischaracterization is corrected, the number of distinct words in Ephesians is not so high, especially since the letter discusses elements of ministry not covered in such detail elsewhere and the letter is less focused on local concerns. This difference in vocabulary is due in part to the fact that Ephesians seems not to have been occasioned by a specific problem in the Ephesian church but was conceived as a regional circular letter. What is more, the amount of special vocabulary in Ephesians is not inordinate but in keeping with the presence of unique vocabulary in Paul's other letters. For example, Ephesians has forty-one words not found elsewhere in the New Testament and eighty-four not found elsewhere in Paul, while the number for Galatians is thirty-five and ninety respectively, a comparable amount.[35] Yet virtually no one doubts that Paul wrote Galatians. Another example is that 2 Corinthians has 5.6 terms used only once in the New Testament per page and Philippians has 6.2, while Ephesians has 4.6 (that is, even slightly less than the other two letters which are widely held to be by Paul). Once again, as in the Pastorals (see test case 3 above), these kinds of numbers tell us that statistics do not solve our question about authorship. To share a quote popularized by Mark Twain, "There are three kinds of lies: lies, damned lies, and statistics."

As far as style is concerned, long sentences are not unique to Ephesians; moreover, the presence of two prayers and a praise psalm may be in play as well in terms of making some sentences longer. To get a better idea of how this all works, compare Romans 8:28–39; 11:8–9; 11:24; 11:25–27; 11:30–31; or 11:33–36 in a section of Romans about as long as the entire letter of Ephesians, or take a look at 1 Corinthians 1:4–8. Many of these sentences have fewer than fifty words, but they are close enough to suggest that length is not a decisive factor.

---

[35] Harold Hoehner, *Ephesians: An Exegetical Commentary* (Grand Rapids: Baker Academic, 2002), 24.

Finally, Ehrman stresses the theological distinctives of this letter as most decisive. Here Ehrman uses three examples: Paul and "works of the flesh," "saved," and "being raised."

- "Works of the flesh": Ehrman argues that Ephesians presents Paul as carried away by lusts of the flesh, apparently citing Ephesians 2:3. Ehrman contrasts this with Paul's claim in Philippians 3:4 that Paul was blameless with reference to the law. He says in effect that the same person cannot have said both things. However, Ehrman fails to note two key points. First, Ephesians 2:1–10 is not strictly a biographical reference but an ethnic reference to Jews and Gentiles. What Ehrman casts as a biographical portrayal of Paul is actually a general remark about Jews in which Paul includes himself as a way of identifying with his readers. This is comparable to Romans 2–3 where he includes Jews—and thus himself— in the scope of guilt that required Christ's work. Second, Ehrman ignores Roman 7, which is cast in the first-person singular and is surely rhetorical. Here Paul declares himself—or whomever the "I" represents—as guilty in terms of the law in that his flesh (i.e., his sinful nature) is not able to fulfill his desire to keep the law. This is similar to the way Paul casts things in Ephesians 2.
- "Saved": Ehrman argues that "saved" conveys only a future sense in Paul. Two observations need to be made here. First, Ehrman views Paul as a rather static theological thinker who is able to express himself in only one way. Yet scholars recognize that Paul was one of the most creative and reflective theological minds in the early church. If Paul was so adept, what makes us think he couldn't develop his thinking in various directions? Does the notion of a theologically fossilized Paul really do justice to such an active mind? This is hardly the case. We should be careful not to confine Paul to a cage of our own making. Second, the idea of having life in the here and now in relation to being saved is not as absent in Paul's writings as Ehrman alleges. In Romans 6, the passage Ehrman cites, Paul uses the picture of baptism to convey the

notion of moving out of death into life. Paul does not intend to say that we die *now* and are raised to life only *later*. Paul intends to say that we die *now* and are raised into life *now*, while awaiting a future resurrection that brings us into everlasting life. Or consider Galatians 2:20, where Paul speaks of the life he *now* lives in Christ.

- "Raised": The previous rubric leads directly to the terminology of "being raised." Is it true that for Paul the notion of resurrection is strictly future so that any present application is un-Pauline? No. In Romans 4:25, Paul says Jesus was "delivered up for our trespasses and raised for our justification." In Romans 3:22–26, Paul ties justification to faith rather than to the end-time future. This shows that for Paul, resurrection is not strictly about the *future* but also has to do with how God delivers a person in response to his or her *present* faith.

This survey has demonstrated that Ehrman has not made a compelling case for New Testament forgeries. He has not even come close. The weaknesses of Ehrman's arguments combine with early church leaders' distaste for pseudonymous activity. The fact that the church had her antennae up to watch for forgeries means the burden of proof continues to remain on the skeptic in proving that forgeries made it into the New Testament.

Claim 4: *Other forms of Christianity are represented in various other writings, which have equally as valid a claim to Christianity as the twenty-seven canonical New Testament books.*

This argument makes the false assumption that there is no way to distinguish between the books included in the New Testament and the books that were excluded. Across the theological spectrum almost all scholars agree that the materials representing divergent forms of Christianity (the apocrypha) are from the second and third centuries. What is more, most of the works carted out in favor of this argument have no conceptual links with the first century. The actual authors of such books attributed their works

to important figures in the early church in order to lend authority
to their writings. In some respects Ehrman seems to be capitaliz-
ing on the recent media attention directed toward the apocryphal
Gospels (such as the *Gospel of Thomas*). Nevertheless, the fact is
that none of the apocryphal Gospels were ever even considered for
inclusion in the New Testament canon. In fact, Cyril of Jerusalem
(fourth century) specifically warns against reading the *Gospel of
Thomas* in the churches (*Catechesis* 6.31); and Origen (second
century) lists *Thomas* as one of the apocryphal heterodox Gospels
(*Hom. in Luc.* 1).

Conversely, the majority of scholars agree that most, if not all,
the New Testament documents were completed by the end of the
first century. Moreover, from the above responses to claims 1–3 it
has become clear that strong evidence exists in favor of trusting
the claims of the New Testament writings to be from an apostle,
someone connected to an apostle, and/or based on eyewitness testimony. What is left is to sketch the characteristics of these later
noncanonical writings to see their lack of historical legitimacy in
comparison with the New Testament. While we cannot interact
with all the apocryphal writings here, the response below provides
a brief survey of the writings that Ehrman implies are equally legitimate with the New Testament writings:

> But where did [the New Testament] come from?
> It came from the victory of the proto-orthodox.
> What if another group had won? What if the New
> Testament contained not Jesus' Sermon on the
> Mount but the Gnostic teachings Jesus delivered
> to his disciples after his resurrection? What if it
> contained not the letters of Paul and Peter but the
> letters of Ptolemy and Barnabas? What if it con-
> tained not the gospels of Matthew, Mark, Luke,
> and John but the Gospels of Thomas, Philip,
> Mary, and Nicodemus?[36]

---

[36] Bart D. Ehrman, *Lost Christianities: The Battles for Scripture and the Faiths We Never Knew*
(Oxford: Oxford University Press, 2003), 248.

1. Letter of Ptolemy[37]

A Gnostic wrote *Ptolemy's Epistle to Flora* in the second century, probably around AD 150–170. Its writer was committed to the form of Gnosticism in which the Old Testament was not from the true God but an intermediate deity, the "Demiurge." The author claimed neither to be an original follower of Jesus nor a companion of an original follower. There is a vast gulf separating the New Testament and the *Letter of Ptolemy* in terms of both date and content.

2. Letter of Barnabas

This letter claims to have been written by Barnabas, the companion of Paul mentioned in the book of Acts. In fact, it was written in the second century by an unknown author. *Barnabas* was a popular book that was at times quoted by certain church fathers, but this does not mean the book was understood to be Scripture.[38] In early Christianity, just as today, pastors and authors read from books other than Scripture and made use of their contents without implying these other works carried the same weight as Scripture.

3. Gospel of Thomas

The *Gospel of Thomas* contains 114 sayings of Jesus. Many of these sayings are strange and esoteric, but some of them sound similar to the words of Jesus found in the canonical Gospels. Several characteristics distinguish *Thomas* from the New Testament Gospels, however. First, *Thomas* has no story line. It includes no account of Jesus' birth, death, or resurrection. Second, the broad consensus is that *Thomas* was written in the middle to late second

---

[37] For a fuller treatment with more extensive notes on each of these writings, see Andreas J. Köstenberger and Michael J. Kruger, *Heresy of Orthodoxy: How Contemporary Culture's Fascination with Diversity Has Reshaped Our Understanding of Early Christianity* (Wheaton: Crossway, 2010), 161–69.

[38] For example, Clement of Alexandria (c. 200) has very high regard for the *Letter of Barnabas*, yet he never calls it "Scripture" and at times is willing to critique it (see *Paed.* 2.10.3; *Strom.* 2.15.67). And though *Barnabas* was included in Claromontanus, a codex dated to the fifth or sixth century, the scribe made a dash beside it, apparently to indicate it was not on the same level as canonical books. The Muratorian canon, Origen, Cyril of Jerusalem, Laodicea, Athanasius, Gregory of Nazianzus, and both the councils of Hippo and Carthage leave *Barnabas* off their canonical lists. Eusebius explicitly lists it as a "rejected" book. For more, see Kruger, *Canon Revisited*, 276–77.

century, much later than the canonical Gospels.[39] Third, at times *Thomas* appears dependent on the New Testament material.[40] As Köstenberger and Kruger conclude,

> It is not surprising, then, that *Thomas* is never mentioned in any early canonical lists, is not found in any of our New Testament manuscript collections, never figured prominently in canonical discussions, and often was condemned outright by a variety of church fathers. Thus, if *Thomas* does represent authentic, original Christianity, then it has left very little historical evidence of that fact.[41]

4. Gospel of Philip

The *Gospel of Philip* was a Gnostic document likely written in the third century, certainly long after the time of the apostles. It shows clear dependence on New Testament material and is structured more as a theological catechism for Gnosticism rather than a historical narrative. *Philip* was never considered in any discussions concerning canonical books. Once again, there is a vast gulf regarding both date and content between the *Gospel of Philip* and the New Testament Gospels.

5. Gospel of Mary

The *Gospel of Mary* is another Gnostic Gospel. It was written in the second century and has no claim of being based on eyewitness testimony. Moreover, it appears to be developing New Testament material for the author's own Gnostic purposes.

---

[39] See, e.g., Nicholas Perrin, *Thomas, the Other Gospel* (Louisville: Westminster John Knox, 2007), and Simon Gathercole, *The Composition of the Gospel of Thomas: Original Language and Influences*, Society for New Testament Studies Monograph Series (Cambridge: Cambridge University Press, 2014).

[40] See Darrell Bock and Daniel Wallace, *Dethroning Jesus: Exposing Popular Culture's Quest to Unseat the Biblical Christ* (Nashville: Thomas Nelson, 2007), 113–22; Gathercole, *Composition of the Gospel of Thomas*.

[41] Köstenberger and Kruger, *Heresy of Orthodoxy*, 166.

6. Gospel of Nicodemus

The *Gospel of Nicodemus* was likely written in the fifth or sixth century. In contrast to the Gospels' narrative of Jesus' life, death, and resurrection, the *Gospel of Nicodemus* tells a fictional story of an interaction between Jesus and Pontius Pilate and of Jesus' actions in hell between his death and resurrection. The *Gospel of Nicodemus* is never mentioned in any canonical discussions, and there are no good reasons for affirming the historical legitimacy of the events described in this book.

This survey makes clear that historical credentials are severely lacking from the apocryphal Gospels and letters mentioned by Ehrman.[42] He leaves the reader with the impression that just about any of these books could have made it into the canon instead of the actual New Testament books. This assumes there is no way of distinguishing between our earliest, best sources to the life of Jesus and the early church (i.e., the New Testament) and later second-century and subsequent sources that lack the historical credentials of the New Testament. The problem with this assumption is that the actual evidence is in stark contradiction to such a proposal.

Once again, for Ehrman, the commitment to seeing diversity has led him to his conclusions despite the lack of evidence he has to support such a story. Strikingly, in his latest work *Did Jesus Exist?* Ehrman seems to concede this point, in glaring contradiction to some of his earliest writings, when he observes, "At the same time, we have nothing to suggest that the beliefs embraced by later Gnostic Christians were present in first-century rural Palestine. And so the Gnostic sayings of Jesus found in such Gnostic Gospels as the Gospel of Philip or the Gospel of Mary almost certainly do

---

[42] To cite just one more piece of evidence against Ehrman's theory, see the recent study by Stanley Porter, "Early Apocryphal Gospels and the New Testament Text," in Charles E. Hill and Michael J. Kruger, eds., *The Early Text of the New Testament* (Oxford: Oxford University Press, 2012), 250–69. Porter examines the *Gospel of Peter*, the *Egerton Papyrus*, *P. Vindobonensis Greek 2325*, *P. Merton II 51*, *P. Oxyrhynchus X 1224*, the *Greek Gospel of Thomas Fragments*, and the *Protevangelium of James*. He concludes that the regular conflation of material from the canonical Gospels and the apparent copying of wording and structure in these apocryphal Gospels suggest that these writings were dependent on the canonical Gospels and that the New Testament text, including that of the canonical Gospels, was well established by the second and third centuries.

not go back to Jesus himself but were placed on his lips by his later (Gnostic) followers."[43]

In closing, it is important to mention an important study by Bruce Metzger—Bart Ehrman's mentor at Princeton—which makes the point that the books that in due course were included in the canon were functioning as authoritative *before* they came to be a part of any canonical list.[44] It was not an authoritative choice of books that gave them their position; instead, authoritative books were already functioning as such and recognized as such.

Claim 5:   *The "proto-orthodox" used the canon as a weapon to impose their own brand of theology on all forms of Christianity and eventually succeeded in the fourth century by way of the powerful church of this period.*

This argument leaves the wrong impression with readers, suggesting that the Christian canon is only a political tool used in service of a power grab by the "proto-orthodox." Nothing could be further from the truth.[45] First, the main thrust of the canon was recognized long before orthodox Christians had the political power to force the heretical books out. While there were some debates concerning the "peripheral" books (e.g., 2 Peter, 2 and 3 John, James, Jude), the "core" was apparently well established by at least the middle of the second century. The canonical lists such as the Muratorian Canon (which most date to around AD 180) or early church leaders such as Irenaeus leave no doubt that only Matthew, Mark, Luke, and John were included in the church's fourfold Gospel canon.[46]

---

[43] Ehrman, *Did Jesus Exist?*, 290.

[44] Bruce M. Metzger, *The Canon of the New Testament* (Oxford: Clarendon, 1987), 282–88.

[45] See the discussion of claim 8 in chapter 4.

[46] See further below. The fragment picks up with Luke and then moves on to John: "at which nevertheless he was present, and so he placed [them in his narrative]. (2) The third book of the Gospel is that according to Luke. (3) Luke, the well-known physician, after the ascension of Christ, (4–5) when Paul had taken with him as one zealous for the law, (6) composed it in his own name, according to [the general] belief. Yet he himself had not (7) seen the Lord in the flesh; and therefore, as he was able to ascertain events, (8) so indeed he begins to tell the story from the birth of John. (9) The fourth of the Gospels is that of John, [one] of the disciples. (10) To his fellow disciples and bishops, who had been urging him [to write], (11) he said, 'Fast with me from today to three days, and what (12) will be revealed to each one (13) let us

Moreover, the Old Testament was a vital part of this "core" set of books from the beginning of the Christian era. Therefore, writings such as those associated with Gnosticism would have been ruled out since they denied the legitimacy of the Old Testament. This core served as a theological boundary against apocryphal and heretical teachings. John Barton writes, "Astonishingly early, the great central core of the present New Testament was already being treated as the main authoritative source for Christians. There is little to suggest that there were any serious controversies about the Synoptics, John, or the major Pauline epistles."[47]

Concerning the New Testament Gospels, Irenaeus (c. AD 180) said, "It is not possible that the Gospels can be either more or fewer in number than they are. For, since there are four zones of the world in which we live and four principal winds, while the church is scattered throughout all the world, and the pillar and ground of the church is the gospel and the spirit of life, it is fitting that she should have four pillars."[48] The Muratorian Fragment— the earliest extant witness to the commonly recognized canonical books (c. AD 180)—also affirms the four New Testament Gospels as the only Gospels.

This makes it likely that the four canonical Gospels were widely established previous to the time of these sayings, which means they were circulating together as Scripture in the beginning to middle of the second century.[49] Similarly, there was impres-

---

tell it to one another.' In the same night it was revealed (14) to Andrew, [one] of the apostles, (15–16) that John should write down all things in his own name while all of them should review it. And so, though various (17) elements may be taught in the individual books of the Gospels, (18) nevertheless this makes no difference to the faith (19) of believers, since by the one sovereign Spirit all things (20) have been declared in all [the Gospels]: concerning the (21) nativity, concerning the passion, concerning the resurrection, (22) concerning life with his disciples, (23) and concerning his twofold coming; (24) the first in lowliness when he was despised, which has taken place, (25) the second glorious in royal power, (26) which is still in the future. What (27) marvel is it then, if John so consistently (28) mentions these particular points also in his Epistles, (29) saying about himself, 'What we have seen with our eyes (30) and heard with our ears and our hands (31) have handled, these things we have written to you?' (32) For in this way he professes [himself] to be not only an eye-witness and hearer, (33) but also a writer of all the marvelous deeds of the Lord, in their order." See Metzger, *The Canon of the New Testament*, 305–7.

[47] John Barton, *The Spirit and the Letter: Studies in the Biblical Canon* (London: SPCK, 1997), 18.

[48] *Haer.* 3.11.8.

[49] See Charles E. Hill, *Who Chose the Gospels? Probing the Great Gospel Conspiracy* (Oxford: Oxford University Press, 2010).

sive early unity in affirming a collection of Paul's letters. Paul's canonical letters were used frequently by the early church fathers, and Irenaeus (c. AD 180) affirms all of Paul's letters included in the New Testament letters except for Philemon. In addition, all thirteen letters traditionally attributed to Paul are listed in the Muratorian Fragment.

Second, Ehrman fails to emphasize that "due to the theological convictions of early Christians about the foundational role of the apostles, there was a built-in sense that the canon was 'closed' after the apostolic time period had ended."[50] From early on, far earlier than the fourth century, the church sought to limit the canon to books from the apostolic time period and to works containing theology consistent with the core doctrines passed to them by the apostles (i.e., the rule of faith; see response to claim 6 in chap. 4). For example, in the Muratorian Fragment of the second century, the *Shepherd of Hermas* is rejected as Scripture because it was "written very recently, in our times."[51] As seen above, for Irenaeus (writing in the late second century) the Gospel canon was "closed" with four. In the early third century, Origen lists all twenty-seven books of the New Testament in a sermon.[52] One last example comes from Dionysius, the bishop of Corinth in the middle of the second century, who distinguished his own letters from the "Scriptures of the Lord."[53] Dionysius believed the Scriptures were a closed entity and no new writings could be included.

In summary, though achieving a universally recognized 27-book closed New Testament canon was a lengthy process, labeling the canon as a "weapon" used by the church to stamp out legitimate diversity conceals more than it reveals. While the canonicity of some peripheral books remained debated in the third

---

[50] Köstenberger and Kruger, *Heresy of Orthodoxy*, 171. See also the works on the canon by Metzger (*Canon of the New Testament*), Bruce (*Canon of Scripture*), and Kruger (*Canon Revisited* and *The Question of Canon*).

[51] "(73) But Hermas wrote the *Shepherd* (74) very recently, in our times, in the city of Rome, (75) while bishop Pius, his brother, was occupying the [episcopal] chair (76) of the church of the city of Rome. (77) And therefore it ought indeed to be read; but (78) it cannot be read publicly to the people in church either among (79) the Prophets, whose number is complete, or among (80) the Apostles, for it is after [their] time" (Metzger's translation; see *Canon of the New Testament*, 305–7).

[52] Köstenberger and Kruger, *Heresy of Orthodoxy*, 172.

[53] Ibid., 173.

and fourth centuries (as they sometimes still are today), by the end of the first century the core books of the New Testament were widely recognized as canonical. This remarkably early recognition of the core books of the canon (especially surprising in light of no formal or universal structure to declare them so) was due to their production during the apostolic period, their connection with the apostles, and their theology that fit within the story and theology of the Old Testament canon.

A League of Their Own

The apocryphal writings were written in the second and third centuries by people who didn't know Jesus or the apostles; this Ehrman does not dispute. Yet he still at times implies that the apocryphal books were as equally legitimate as the New Testament documents and could have been included in the canon. The only way he can make such a claim is by demonstrating that the New Testament writings are similar to these apocryphal writings. This is where the argument of forgery fits into Ehrman's picture of early Christian writings: the New Testament writings are not that much different from these other later writings because, after all, the New Testament was also forged. Yet, collectively, the arguments in this chapter have shown that these apocryphal writings are not even in the same league, as far as historical credentials go, as the New Testament. Apparently, at times even Ehrman is willing to admit this. In 2011, he wrote,

> [I]f historians want to know what Jesus said and did they are more or less constrained to use the New Testament Gospels as their principal sources. Let me emphasize that this is not for religious or theological reasons—for instance, that these and these alone can be trusted. It is for historical reasons, pure and simple. . . . Moreover, the Gospel accounts outside the New Testament tend to be late and legendary . . . of little use to the historian interested in knowing what happened during Jesus' lifetime. . . . [T]he only real sources

available to the historian interested in the life of Jesus are therefore the New Testament Gospels.[54]

On this point Ehrman is correct. Historically, the New Testament Gospels—and we would add, the entire New Testament—are in a league of their own.

Discussion Questions

1. Discuss the significance of Richard Bauckham's conclusion that the Gospels were based on eyewitness testimony. How does Bauckham's work undercut many of the assumptions of critical scholars?
2. List the evidence that contradicts the claim that Peter was "a backwoods illiterate peasant" (Ehrman, *Forged*, 75).
3. Explain the correct interpretation of *agrammatoi* in Acts 4:13.
4. Discuss the merits for the traditionally held authorship of 1 Peter, 2 Peter, 2 Thessalonians, and Ephesians.
5. Describe some of the differences between the canonical books and books not accepted into the canon.

---

[54] Ehrman, *New Testament: A Historical Introduction*, 215.

CONCLUSION: REASONS TO BELIEVE

Can We Trust the Bible?

Can the Bible be trusted? Ehrman, as well as other critics, answers with a resounding no! They insist that the Bible's difficulties are so extensive that skepticism is the only reasonable conclusion for an unbiased scholar. However, this is simply not the case. This is not to say there aren't difficulties in the Bible—such as apparent chronological differences and theological tensions—but as one scholar noted more than twenty-five years ago, "The difficulties raised by the biblical phenomena are on the whole a good deal less intractable than is sometimes suggested."[1] That this quote was penned in the mid-1980s reminds us that Ehrman's critiques are not new; conservative scholars have long been offering thoughtful responses. Nevertheless, the church to a large part has not sufficiently taken note of and passed down the historical and theological knowledge that builds a foundation for a reasonable faith. Into this environment Ehrman has entered. He has found an audience among past and present churchgoers, some of them skeptics, many of whom are interested, shocked,

---

[1] D. A. Carson, "Recent Developments in the Doctrine of Scripture," in *Hermeneutics, Authority, and Canon*, ed. D. A. Carson and John D. Woodbridge (Grand Rapids: Zondervan, 1986), 23.

and left wondering why they have never learned any of this in their churches.

Despite the anxiety Ehrman's rhetoric can produce, however, in some ways he has done all of us a favor. He has focused discussion on topics to which everyday Christians and pastors have given inadequate attention for too long. In highlighting these issues for the masses, Ehrman opens the door for new conversations to arise over the historicity and reliability of the Bible. Church leaders and teachers must rise to the occasion and be prepared to serve as tour guides through these issues. Christians have nothing to fear by taking a closer look at the evidence, and unbelieving seekers are not required to take a blind leap of faith.

We have seen that Ehrman's objections are not only refutable (and many of the so-called problems are not that problematic after all) but also that Ehrman's arguments at times even end up working against each other. For instance, Ehrman frequently argues heresy has as equal claim as Christianity to orthodoxy in the early church. In making this argument, he notes that our New Testament canon could have easily included Gnostic texts. However, as we pointed out in chapter 5, Ehrman, in *Did Jesus Exist?*, writes, "[W]e have nothing to suggest that the beliefs embraced by later Gnostic Christians were present in first-century rural Palestine. And so the Gnostic sayings of Jesus found in such Gnostic Gospels as the Gospel of Philip or the Gospel of Mary almost certainly do not go back to Jesus himself but were placed on his lips by his later (Gnostic) followers."[2] This statement is helpful to his argument in *Did Jesus Exist?* as he sets out to defend the historicity of Jesus, but it is contradictory to his views on early Christianity expressed in other places.[3] Or, to give but one other example, we have explained

---

[2] Bart D. Ehrman, *Did Jesus Exist? The Historical Argument for Jesus of Nazareth* (San Francisco: HarperOne, 2012), 290.

[3] For example, see Bart D. Ehrman, *Lost Christianities: The Battles for Scripture and the Faiths We Never Knew* (Oxford: Oxford University Press, 2003), 248: "But where did [the New Testament] come from? It came from the victory of the proto-orthodox. What if another group had won? What if the New Testament contained not Jesus' Sermon on the Mount but the Gnostic teachings Jesus delivered to his disciples after his resurrection? What if it contained not the letters of Paul and Peter but the letters of Ptolemy and Barnabas? What if it contained not the gospels of Matthew, Mark, Luke, and John but the Gospels of Thomas, Philip, Mary, and Nicodemus?"

how Ehrman, on the one hand, seeks to undermine confidence in the reliability of the copying of the New Testament text. Yet, on the other hand, in different writings he seeks to reconstruct a historical Jesus primarily from the wording in the canonical Gospels and even adds,

> [T]he problem is not of such a scope as to make it impossible to have any idea what the ancient Christian authors wrote. If we had no clue what was originally in the writings of Paul or in the Gospels, this objection might carry more weight. But there is not a textual critic on the planet who thinks this, since not a shred of evidence leads in this direction.[4]

At times it seems the interpretation of the same evidence changes, depending on whom Ehrman is debating.

Ehrman portrays his early days as a fundamentalist as being filled with plenty of passion but precious little knowledge. In due course, says Ehrman, he reached the point where he courageously looked the evidence in the face and admitted the Bible is not to be trusted. While clearly many of his core beliefs have changed since his fundamentalist days, Ehrman's expectations for what the Bible *must be* in order for it to be considered inspired have apparently not changed all that much. In fact, it appears he has set the bar intentionally so high that no one will ever be able to satisfy his demands for sufficient evidence for faith. For example, despite the New Testament manuscript evidence being far superior to any work of antiquity, this is not enough for Ehrman. Despite the core theological truths that run through the writings of the various authors of the New Testament and the legitimate diversity within these books, Ehrman sees theological contradictions. While the Bible offers multifaceted answers to the question of evil, including a call for dependence on a transcendent God who maintains it as his divine prerogative to keep some reasons a mystery, Ehrman says this is simply not good enough. There is a fine line between

---

[4] Ehrman, *Did Jesus Exist?*, 181.

credulity and skepticism, and it appears at times that, ironically, Ehrman's instincts to see things in black and white, rather than sufficiently nuanced, have caused him to pass from one extreme to the other.

In answering Ehrman's objections to faith in the God and Jesus revealed in the Bible, we have observed numerous reasons to believe. From the vast and early manuscript evidence to the remarkable unity amid the diverse New Testament authors and genres, Ehrman's objections, once explored, point us to evidence in support of Scripture. However, "Evidence in support is one thing," you might be saying, "but I need proof!" *Proof* can be a tricky term. If someone asks for "proof" of your identity, you can pull out your driver's license or some kind of ID. This will pretty much settle things. Assuming we are not dealing with fake IDs, certain things such as proving identity or hair color or height are fairly easy to verify. Even with these types of things that seem easy to prove, there are ways that motivated and clever people can trick others; but for the most part we accept as true the things we can personally observe.

Our point is that "proof" or evidence is rarely a case of 100 percent shown. We are reminded of the court case where the accused person's DNA is found on the scene sitting by the victim's body. An attorney defending his client and seeking to get him declared innocent will raise all kinds of hypothetical questions. How do we know the DNA was laid down at the time of the murder? After all, DNA doesn't come with a date stamp on it like some photographs. Maybe the way the DNA was collected was sloppy and led to a wrong result. A jury doesn't have the luxury of 100 percent proof, and yet they render a verdict. Historical disputes are of a similar character. We don't prove the result or "prove" the Bible. What one can show is that trust in Scripture is reasonable, and an argument that makes sense can be made, just like finding the DNA of the murderer by the victim at a crime scene leads to a likely conclusion the accused is guilty.

With regard to the past, one cannot empirically prove a historical event in the same way in which one proves a mathematical equation or verifies that someone is six feet tall or has blue eyes, though historical evidence can point strongly in one direction. Historical truths are tested by assessing hypotheses in view of the evidence and then accepting the hypothesis that best explains the evidence. So it is widely held that George Washington was the first president of the United States, but you can't prove this by observation. You must rely on eyewitnesses and the credibility of written accounts. Of course, it is just possible that a grand conspiracy took place and George Washington was a mythical figure and all the accounts of his presidency and perhaps even his existence were made up, though this seems highly unlikely. Thus, while historical proof is different from mathematical proof, historical evidence can be compelling and inspire confident assent.

The Origins for Christianity

One of the central historical questions we have yet to address in our responses to Ehrman is how this tiny offshoot of Judaism, which subsequently went on to change the world, originated. Unfortunately, Ehrman's chosen overall stance of doubt has hampered his ability to provide an adequate historical explanation for Christianity. For instance, he writes about what happened after Jesus' death: "But then something else happened. Some of them began to say that God had intervened and brought him back from the dead. The story caught on, and some (or all—we don't know) of his closest followers came to think that in fact he had been raised."[5] And again, "For some reason, however, the followers of Jesus (or at least some of them) came to think he had been raised from the dead."[6] But why would they say such a thing? What is the most credible historical explanation?

While Ehrman accepts that the disciples came to believe Jesus was resurrected, in his most recent book, *How Jesus Became God*, he seeks to explain away the empty tomb by arguing that there was no known tomb to begin with.[7] But is this really historically credible? Craig Evans has recently shown that it isn't.[8] As Evans

---

[5] Ibid., 164.

[6] Ibid., 233.

[7] Bart D. Ehrman, *How Jesus Became God: The Exaltation of a Jewish Preacher from Galilee* (San Francisco: HarperCollins, 2014), 129–69.

[8] Craig A. Evans, "Getting the Burial Traditions and Evidences Right," in *How God Became*

points out and as you'll see below, not only is Ehrman selective in his use of the available historical evidence, he lodges a fallacious argument from the silence of a creed and completely ignores important archaeological evidence.

Ehrman attempts to defend this claim by pointing out that neither Joseph of Arimathea—the man who placed Jesus in the tomb according to the Gospels—nor the tomb itself was ever mentioned in the earliest creed (1 Cor. 15:3b–5a). Yet, 1 Corinthians 15:4 does say, "He was buried." What did Paul think Jesus was buried in? Moreover, since Paul follows "He was buried" in the same verse with the affirmation, "He was raised," the obvious historical conclusion is that whatever Jesus was buried in, presumably a tomb, was now empty.

What is more, the mere lack of specific reference to Joseph of Arimathea must not be construed to imply that Paul and the creed deny the event happened. Creeds are meant to be *condensed* expressions of faith, not exhaustive and detailed historical accounts. Who saw the risen Jesus is an important issue in 1 Corinthians 15, but, as Evans points out, "*Who buried Jesus was not*."[9] Just imagine yourself affirming a statement of faith and then someone coming along and pointing out all the things you did not include and then saying just because you didn't exhaustively list all of your beliefs, you therefore don't believe certain things that are not in your statement. You would likely respond that this critique is invalid and based on undue skepticism. And you would be right!

Also, Ehrman argues that Roman policy didn't allow the crucified to be buried. There is some truth to this *in certain contexts*, but because Ehrman hasn't provided the reader with all the historical evidence, he ends up concealing more than he reveals. In *some* parts of the Roman Empire and especially during wartime, the bodies of those executed were indeed regularly left on their crosses to rot or to be eaten by animals. But if this were the normal way the Romans treated the Jews in and around Jerusalem, why did the Romans and the Jews not simply reply to the Christian claim

---

Jesus: The Real Origins of Belief in Jesus' Divine Nature: A Response to Bart D. Ehrman, ed. Michael F. Bird (Grand Rapids: Zondervan, 2014), 71–93.

   [9] Ibid., 91 (emphasis added).

that there was an empty tomb on these terms: "*Of course* there is no body in the tomb because *he was never allowed to be buried*"? That would have been the proper response to the claim of resurrection and an empty tomb. Yet, that is not how people commonly responded, apparently because it was common knowledge that the Romans normally allowed the Jews to bury their dead. Instead, the story was circulated that the body had been stolen, which would not have happened unless the body was actually missing. The idea that a stolen body story was made up by the church and added later is hardly credible since to misreport the reaction to the claim of an empty tomb would seriously undercut the credibility of the claim in the first place.

Evans demonstrates, with reference to Philo and Josephus among various other sources, that in peacetime Jerusalem (and just outside its walls), with its unique political and social situation, the Roman administration seems to have normally respected Jewish burial customs for the executed.[10] For example, Philo points out the expectation, due to common past practice, for the Romans to respect Jewish customs: the Jews "appealed to Pilate to redress the infringement of their traditions caused by the shields and *not to disturb the customs which throughout all the preceding ages had been safeguarded without disturbance by kings and by emperors*."[11] To cite just one more example from Evans, "The Jewish historian and apologist [Josephus] adds that the Roman procurators who succeeded Agrippa I 'by abstaining from interface with the customs of the country kept the nation at peace' (*Jewish War* 2.220), customs that included never leaving a 'corpse unburied' (*Against Apion*, 2.211). Had Roman governors—in Israel, especially in the vicinity of Jerusalem itself—regularly crucified Jews and left their bodies hanging on crosses, it is unlikely they would have 'kept the nation at peace.'"[12]

Finally, the archeological evidence, which Ehrman fails to include, supports the contention that in Palestine the Romans often allowed for the crucified to be buried. In a survey of the

---

[10] Ibid., 83–89.
[11] Ibid., 77.
[12] Ibid., 77–78.

archeological evidence, Evans cites how certain human remains, which had been given proper burial around Jesus' time, show signs of Roman execution. To mention just one specific example from several Evans cites, a discovery was made in 1968 (more than 40 years ago, hardly breaking news), of an ossuary (ossuary no. 4 in Tomb I, at Giv'at ha-Mivtar) with a crucified Jewish man by the name of Yehohanan.[13] He also notes the dozens of, perhaps even more than one hundred, nails that have been found in tombs and ossuaries. Some of these nails include traces of human calcium, indicating their likely use in crucifixion. In summary, Evans cites Jodi Magness, a Jewish archeologist at UNC Chapel Hill:

> Gospel accounts of Jesus' burial are largely con-
> sistent with the archeological evidence. Although
> archaeology does not prove there was a follower
> of Jesus named Joseph of Arimathea or that
> Pontius Pilate granted his request for Jesus' body,
> *the Gospel account describing Jesus' removal from*
> *the cross and burial are consistent with archaeolog-*
> *ical evidence and with Jewish law.*[14]

Ehrman accepts that Jesus' disciples "came to think that in fact he had been raised from the dead." His argument against the burial of Jesus once again highlights Ehrman's way of at times telling only part of the story. That the resurrection account caught on is further evidence that this known tomb must have been empty. After all, the claim would have been quickly disproven if Jesus' body had been found and put on display. Initially skeptical followers might have checked the claim out. And there indeed was a deep desire among the Christians' opponents to end all this resurrection talk. But, no corpse was ever produced. All the canonical Gospels as well as Paul attest to an empty tomb. Even the Jewish leaders, though refusing to acknowledge Jesus' resurrection, did not deny that Jesus' tomb was empty. Again, Evans writes, "The whereabouts of the place

---

[13] Ibid., 83–85.
[14] Ibid., 89; cf. J. Magness, "Jesus' Tomb: What Did It Look Like?", in *Where Christianity Was Born,* ed. H. Shanks (Washington, DC: Biblical Archeology Society, 2006), 224 (emphasis added).

where Jesus' corpse was interred would have been known. No matter what people said about seeing the risen Jesus, the place of burial would have remained important. Had his corpse remained in the tomb, that would have been known and its eventual retrieval for burial in an honorable place . . . would have been planned."[15] But, of course, no corpse was ever retrieved!

Since Christianity began because of an empty tomb and because of Jesus' earliest followers' claim that Jesus was raised from the dead, what is the best historical explanation for this proclamation and the tomb with no body? We will get to some other possible explanations soon, but it is important to stop and consider the significance of the Christian claim that the best historical explanation for these two facts is that Jesus actually did rise from the dead. In some measure the starting point for a decision on Christianity— and perhaps the ending point for those who remain skeptical—can be put as simply as this: Did Jesus rise from the dead? If he didn't, you shouldn't become a Christian. What is more, as Paul has noted in 1 Corinthians 15, if that is the case, you'd have every right to feel sorry for Christians who believe in a lie. But if Jesus really did come back to life from the dead, this changes everything.

For some reading this book and for some with whom you will talk, the greatest challenge to accepting Christianity is not textual variants or the diversity of the early church but rather the question of the supernatural. In other words, can modern people well acquainted with the basics of science accept the reliability of documents filled with stories of miracles? This question has more to do with one's worldview than it does with any deficiency in the New Testament itself. If there is a God who created the world, as the Bible claims, then miracles caused by this God are not only possible; they are to be expected.[16] However, if one argues that miracles cannot happen because there is no God, and therefore the Bible is false and Jesus did not rise from the dead, he has only come full circle in his argument. Arguing that the Bible cannot be true because miracles cannot happen is sort of like arguing the earth

---

[15] Evans, "Getting the Burial Traditions and Evidences Right," 92–93.

[16] See Craig S. Keener, *Miracles: The Credibility of the New Testament Accounts*, 2 vols. (Grand Rapids: Baker, 2011).

cannot revolve around the sun because everyone knows the sun revolves around the earth. Once you allow historical evidence to point you forward rather than holding a prior bias against miracles, the evidence is amazingly strong for a bodily resurrection of Jesus. As an approach to looking at some of this evidence, we will survey two of the most commonly held alternative explanations.

Some, such as Ehrman recently, have claimed that the disciples likely simply hallucinated. Several factors make such an explanation unreasonable. First, while hallucinations do occur, since the disciples, Paul, James (the brother of Jesus), and at one time more than 500 people claimed to have seen the resurrected Jesus, they would all have had to experience the same hallucination of the risen Jesus, and in some cases simultaneously.[17] Second, while it has been argued that Jesus' followers were in such a state of grief that they hallucinated, this would hardly explain why Paul, a committed Jewish leader who was persecuting Christians and clearly not grieving, would have hallucinated. Third, the hallucination theory does not explain why the tomb was empty.[18]

Others have claimed that the disciples simply made up the whole resurrection story. They wanted Jesus to be the Messiah so

---

[17] Ehrman thinks we can only be sure about three or possibly four early followers (Peter, Paul, Mary Magdalene, and possibly James, the brother of Jesus) having these encounters with someone they at least thought was Jesus (*How Jesus Became God*, 192). He suggests that Paul's statement that more than 500 hundred people saw the resurrected Jesus cannot be trusted (*How Jesus Became God*, 202; cf. 1 Cor. 15:5–8). However, Paul adds that this appearance to the large group was just one of many times people saw Jesus and that many of these more than 500 witnesses were still alive, which meant Paul's claim could have easily been invalidated if these witnesses weren't really around. And not only this, the Gospels and Acts are also in agreement that Christ appeared to more than just three or four people. However, even if for argument's sake we accept Ehrman's claim that we can be confident only that three or four people believed they saw Jesus, why would Paul have this hallucination? Certainly, for pre-conversion Paul, who was no friend of Jesus or his followers, it was not induced by grief, as Ehrman suggests as a possible cause for these hallucinations. What is more, for Ehrman's argument to work, not only would Paul have had to have a vision that we have no indication he was expecting, Mary Magdalene, Peter, and James would have had to have the same hallucination at different times. It is understandable for one to make such strained proposals if the miraculous is ruled out as a possible explanation *a priori*, but if the historian remains open to the possibility of divine intervention, though it can't be "proven," the resurrection makes the most sense out of the evidence for transformation of views. Finally, if these four witnesses are so crucial (Peter, Paul, Mary Magdalene, and possibly James) and it was so easy to add stories and embellish the traditions as Ehrman claims, why do we never get a detailed account of the appearances to Peter or James? In the end, the evidence implies that the biblical tradition was careful about what it passed on and did not invent things on the fly for apologetic reasons.

[18] See the above section on the empty tomb, on page 167.

badly and were so disappointed after his death that they concocted this grand hoax. They stole the body of Jesus and then claimed Jesus really was the Messiah and that he had been resurrected from the dead. Yet this theory cannot hold any water either.

First, it makes no sense that the disciples would make up a story that claims Jesus is the Messiah because he was shamefully crucified and then was raised from the dead, since this was not the common expectation for the Jewish Messiah. Ehrman himself makes the point that Jesus did not meet the expectations that first-century Jews had regarding the Messiah:

> Ancient Judaism (before Christianity) never did have an idea that the messiah would suffer for others—that's why the vast majority of Jews rejected the idea that Jesus could be the messiah. The messiah was to be a figure of grandeur and power—for example, someone like the mighty King David—who would rule over God's people. And who was Jesus? A crucified criminal, just the opposite of what the messiah would be.[19]

Ehrman is certainly right at this point. And this is why in the Gospels, when Jesus tells his disciples that he would be killed and then would rise again, the disciples do not comprehend his predictions. All the Gospels describe the disciples as repeatedly failing to understand Jesus' statements concerning his death, burial, and resurrection. Though the Old Testament anticipated the coming of the Messiah and the events surrounding his death and resurrection, the disciples were slow to understand. This was because apparently the disciples, along with other first-century Jews, believed the Messiah would serve as a national deliverer, engage in military conquest, and set up a kingdom on earth—not die on a cross and subsequently be resurrected from the grave.

In fact, because of these expectations regarding the Messiah and because of the prevailing culture's worldview, it would have

---

[19] Bart D. Ehrman, *God's Problem: How the Bible Fails to Answer Our Most Important Question—Why We Suffer* (New York: HarperCollins, 2008), 82.

been difficult for people to accept the resurrection of Jesus. The dominant view in non-Jewish thought was that bodily resurrection was impossible because of the belief that the soul was good and the physical body was bad. In this view the separation of the soul from the body at death was positive, and a bodily resurrection was not only unheard of; it was undesirable. Jews did hope for a future bodily resurrection; however, this resurrection was seen as only part of a future bodily resurrection of *all the righteous*, not just one particular person.[20] What is more, this future resurrection was thought to occur along with the renewal of the entire world. Jews were not expecting an individual to be resurrected in the middle of history while the problems of the world continued to unfold. As one recent author put it, "If some had said to any first-century Jew, 'So-and-so has been resurrected from the dead!' the response would be, 'Are you crazy? How could that be? Has disease and death ended? Is true justice established in the world? Has the wolf lain down with the lamb? Ridiculous!'"[21] The idea that the disciples would have made up the story of Jesus' resurrection assumes people were expecting the Messiah first to be killed and then to rise from the dead or were at least open to the idea, but this just isn't the case.[22]

In fact, we know from history that Jesus was not the first person who gathered a following among those who believed him to be the Messiah and was subsequently executed. Nevertheless,

> In not one single case do we hear the slightest mention of the disappointed followers claiming that

---

[20] It misses the point to cite instances such as when Lazarus was resuscitated from the dead and when Herod Antipas believed that Jesus was John the Baptist "raised from the dead" as evidence that individual resurrections fit within the prevailing Jewish worldview. These examples are different from the claim concerning Jesus' resurrection. Jesus did not rise from the dead only to one day grow old and die again. Instead, the claim being made in the case of Jesus was that he was resurrected to an eternal glorified body. This type of resurrection from the dead was expected to occur at the renewal of the entire world as a corporate and universal event rather than an individual one. Ehrman seems to understand this point (*How Jesus Became God*, 205), and hence the problem with claiming that the disciples simply made it up: it was not something they would have expected to happen, nor was it something they would have expected others to easily accept.

[21] Timothy Keller, *The Reason for God: Belief in an Age of Skepticism* (New York: Penguin, 2008), 215–16.

[22] For an extensive work on the Jewish and non-Jewish worldview concerning resurrection see N. T. Wright, *The Resurrection of the Son of God* (Minneapolis: Fortress, 2003).

their hero had been raised from the dead. They knew better. Resurrection was not a private event. Jewish revolutionaries whose leader had been executed by the authorities, and who managed to escape arrest themselves, had two options: give up the revolution or find another leader. Claiming that the original leader was alive again was simply not an option. Unless, of course, he was.[23]

What is more, if the disciples made up such a claim, it seems impossible to believe that they would have carried their hoax so far, being severely persecuted and in many cases giving up their lives for what they knew was a lie they themselves had concocted.[24] As Gary Habermas has noted,

Virtually no one, friend, or foe, believer or critic, denies that it was their convictions that they had seen the resurrected Jesus that caused the disciples' radical transformations. They were willing to die *specifically for their resurrection belief.* Down through the centuries many have been willing to give their lives for political or religious cause. But

---

[23] N. T. Wright, *Who Was Jesus?* (Grand Rapids: Eerdmans, 1993), 63.

[24] In trying to counter this point, Ehrman denies that we can "know what happened to most disciples in the end" and concludes, "So there is no need for talk about dying for a lie" (*How Jesus Became God*, 165). However, he fails to give any evidence against the tradition that many of the first eyewitnesses were martyred and misses the main point of this argument. There is overwhelming evidence that the apostles and early Christians were persecuted for their beliefs. Stephen was stoned (Acts 6–8), Herod Agrippa killed James, the brother of John (Acts 12:2; supported by Josephus, *Antiquities* 20.200), and Nero sponsored the first statewide persecution in the early 60s (see Tacitus, *Annals* 15.37–41). Paul recounts how he experienced grueling persecution (2 Cor 6:4–9), and most scholars accept the tradition that he was martyred in the 60s (*1 Clem.* 5:5–7; Eusebius, *Hist. eccl.* 2.25.5–8). According to Acts 5:17–42, Peter and John were thrown into prison and flogged. John 21:18–19 implies that it was well known by the time of John's Gospel that Peter died as a martyr. Eckhard J. Schnabel, *Early Christian Mission*, 2 vols. (Downers Grove: InterVarsity, 2004), 1533–38, documents some of the persecution the early Christians experienced, and to our point, it is difficult to see why Jesus' earliest followers would have been willing to undergo such experiences if they knew themselves to be suffering for a lie. In an aside, Ehrman claims that in any case people have indeed given up their lives for what they knew to be a lie when they thought "it would serve the greater good" (*How Jesus Became God*, 165). Yet, this makes little sense in the case of the earliest disciples. After all, how would people benefit by believing Jesus had risen from the dead if indeed he hadn't? In fact, Paul says the exact opposite in 1 Corinthians 15 when he argues that if Jesus did not really rise from the dead, people who believe this are most of all to be "pitied" (v. 19).

the crucial difference here is that while many have died for their *convictions*, Jesus' disciples were in the right place to know the truth or falsity of the event for which they were willing to die.[25]

If someone is going to deny the resurrection, he or she must be able to explain "how a small band of defeated followers of Jesus were transformed almost overnight into bold witnesses, risking death by proclaiming his bodily resurrection before many of the same people who fifty days earlier had participated in his crucifixion."[26] Remember, the alternative view is that someone had to make up the idea of a raised Jesus. A fair question is, Where would that have come from? There was no precedent in Judaism for a raised Messiah to create this idea or even look for it. In Jewish faith, resurrection was something that happens to all at the end of history. So there is no real context to generate such a view unless there was a real impulse in an actual event (Jesus' resurrection!) to create this new idea.

Third, that all four Gospels have women as the first eyewitnesses to the resurrection stands against those who claim these accounts are mythical legends produced by the disciples. If first-century Jews were going to make up a story, it would be counterintuitive to make women the first eyewitnesses. In this culture women were not permitted to testify in a court of law.[27] The fact that all four Gospels include women as the first eyewitnesses points to the historicity of the resurrection. After all, if the Gospel writers were simply inventing the stories of the resurrection, surely they would have invented male witnesses as the first to report the empty tomb. A man's testimony was viewed as reliable and would stand up in court, but all four Gospels have women as the first

---

[25] Gary R. Habermas, "The Resurrection Appearances of Jesus," in *Evidence for God*, 174–75.

[26] Craig L. Blomberg, "Jesus of Nazareth: How Historians Can Know Him and Why It Matters," accessed June 30, 2012, http://thegospelcoalition.org/cci/article/jesus_of_nazareth_how_historians_can_know_him_and_why_it_matters.

[27] Richard Bauckham, *Gospel Women: Studies of the Named Women in the Gospels* (Grand Rapids: Eerdmans/Edinburgh: T&T Clark, 2002), 268–77; cf. Wright, *Resurrection of the Son of God*, 607. See also ancient Jewish texts such as *m. Shebuot* 4.1; *Rosh Hashanah* 1.8; *b. Baba Qamma* 88a that show how consistent this idea was across the centuries of Jewish tradition, even after the time of Jesus.

witnesses, the most reasonable explanation being that this is the way it actually happened.[28]

We also have to explain the mocking the leaders of the church gave the women who originally reported the empty tomb. The church would never make up a story that went this way. This is not the way to commend your leaders who are arguing for a difficult cultural idea like resurrection.

Finally, the alternative model says you create scenes involving luminaries to buttress the credibility of the made-up story or of a source otherwise unknown. Yet we do not have a report in the tradition of Jesus' appearance to Peter alone or James alone. If one were making up such stories and multiplying them, why do we not have such a detailed account when the tradition knows of such appearances? This shows how carefully and circumspectly the tradition was passed on. There are no additions of the type we might expect if the stories were created to make an impression.

This is just some of the evidence that has led numerous historians who are unwilling to exclude the possibility of the miraculous to conclude, along similar lines as N. T. Wright has articulated, "The historian may and must say that all other explanations for why Christianity arose, and why it took the shape it did, are far less convincing as historical explanations than the one the early Christians themselves offer: that Jesus really did rise from the dead on Easter morning, leaving an empty tomb behind him."[29]

---

[28] Ehrman attempts to undermine this point by noting that these traditions were not being tried in a court of law so the disallowance of women's testimony in a court of law is invalid. Yet, Ehrman overlooks that the illegitimacy of women's testimony in a court of law is actually an example of a wider phenomenon in the culture in which women were not seen as giving trustworthy testimony on important matters. In this circumstance, it is the public setting that counts the most. Ehrman goes further by arguing that women could have made up these traditions to give themselves a prominent role in the resurrection stories. Yet, the idea that female self-promotion gives the answer to why women are in all the Gospel traditions as the first eyewitnesses to the resurrection misses the point and serves as a red herring. The real issue is how the public would respond to an unpopular doctrine being promulgated by people who did not culturally count as witnesses. No one trying to keep hope alive would have invented it this way, as it would not have been persuasive. As Evans points out, "If the gospel stories were filled with as much fiction as Ehrman thinks, one must wonder why the Evangelists did not alter the stories and give more prominence to men" ("Getting the Burial Traditions and Evidences Right," 90). All this strongly suggests the women were in the story because they were in the event.

[29] N. T. Wright, "Jesus' Resurrection and Christian Origins," accessed June 30, 2012, http://ntwrightpage.com/Wright_Jesus_Resurrection.htm. For more evidence for the resurrection, see Wright, *Resurrection of the Son of God*; and Gary R. Habermas and Michael R. Licona, *The Case for the Resurrection of Jesus* (Grand Rapids: Kregel, 2004).

Indeed, the most reasonable conclusion from the evidence is that Jesus did rise from the dead. Tim Keller writes of how this truth changes everything:

> Each year at Easter I get to preach on the Resurrection. In my sermon I always say to my skeptical, secular friends, that even if they can't believe in the resurrection, they should want it to be true. Most of them care deeply about justice for the poor, alleviating hunger and disease, and caring for the environment. Yet, many of them believe that the material world was caused by accident and that the world and everything in it will eventually simply burn up in the death of the sun. They find it discouraging that so few people care about justice without realizing that their own worldview undermines any motivation to make the world a better place. Why sacrifice for the needs of others if in the end nothing we do will make any differences? If the resurrection of Jesus happened, however, that means there's infinite hope and reason to pour ourselves out for the needs of the world.[30]

Taking up the Challenge

Ehrman tells the following story of how he often begins his university classes:

> The first day of class, with over three hundred students present, I ask: "How many of you would agree with the proposition that the Bible is the inspired Word of God?" *Whoosh!* Virtually everyone in the auditorium raises their hand. I then ask, "How many of you have one or more of the Harry Potter books?" *Whoosh!* The whole auditorium.

---

[30] Keller, *Reason for God*, 220.

> Then I ask, "And how many of you have read the
> entire Bible?" Scattered hands, a few students
> here and there. I always laugh and say, "Okay,
> look. I'm not saying that I think God wrote the
> Bible. You're telling me that you think God wrote
> the Bible. I can see why you might want to read a
> book by J. K. Rowling. But if God wrote a book
> . . . wouldn't you want to see what he has to say?"[31]

We couldn't have made the point better ourselves! The challenge for everyone who thinks the Bible is, or even is possibly, inspired by God is to actually read it.

We have trusted in Jesus not *just* because we have formed and accepted the arguments in this book. Indeed, we think that the case for the Bible and the Christian faith is altogether much more convincing than the case for skepticism. Yet, in each of our lives, we also have had powerful experiences with God as we began to understand more of the teachings of the Bible. And the more we have rigorously studied the Bible, the more our faith has grown.

Our hope is this book has equipped you to give people the reasons why they should shed their skepticism and the doubts of the surrounding culture to give the Bible a chance so that they might experience the power of the God who inspired it.

Discussion Questions

1. How has reading this book helped you understand better some of the legitimate answers to the questions raised by skeptics?
2. Do you still have any remaining unresolved questions? If so, what are they?
3. Are you reading the Bible on a regular basis? If not, what is keeping you from doing so? How can you do better in this regard?

---

[31] Bart D. Ehrman, *Jesus, Interrupted: Revealing the Hidden Contradictions in the Bible (And Why We Don't Know about Them)* (San Francisco: HarperOne, 2009), 225–26.

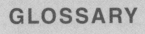

GLOSSARY

Autographs　　　The original Old and New Testament documents that are now lost but whose text is available in an abundance of manuscripts.

The Bauer Thesis　The theory that the traditional form of Christianity (i.e., orthodoxy) was actually nothing but the view that was imposed by one early Christian sect onto the rest of Christendom.

Canon　　　　　A group of recognized authoritative texts.

Church fathers　　Leaders in the generations after the apostles who were influential in the early church.

Codex　　　　　In contrast to scrolls, the codex looks similar to modern-day books and was a new invention during the days of the early church. The codex found widespread and early acceptance as the preferred instrument for recording Christian literature.

Dead Sea community　A community living in the time of Jesus on the northwestern shore of the Dead Sea. We know this community most directly through the discovery of the Dead Sea Scrolls.

External evidence　Data indicating the quality of a particular manuscript.

Form criticism　　An approach that has often assumed the Gospels were folk literature passed down by people with no interest in history who changed the traditions of Jesus to fit their particular purpose.

Gnosticism　　　A label for various second-century heretical groups that commonly held such things as an emphasis on secret knowledge, a negative view of the physical world, and a denial of the humanity of Jesus.

Heresy	Teaching regarding Jesus that deviates from standard norms of Christian doctrine.
***Inclusio* of eyewitness testimony**	The practice of identifying a primary witness at the beginning and the end of a work. This is seen in Mark's Gospel when he identifies Peter at the beginning and at the end of his Gospel.
Internal evidence	Data supplied by the context of a particular passage that contains the variant.
Irenaeus	Early church leader who has left us testimony concerning the New Testament canon.
Legitimate diversity	Diversity that does not involve contradiction.
Manuscripts	Copies made by hand.
Multifunctional scribes	Professional scribes trained in copying both documentary and literary texts.
Muratorian Canon	A list of authoritative Christian books from around AD 180. This is the earliest witness to the canonical books included in the New Testament.
Nomina Sacra	Abbreviations in the New Testament for common words such as "God" and "Lord." These abbreviations are significant because they appear in the earliest manuscripts, are exclusive to Christianity, and are widespread across regions and languages.
Orthodoxy	Correct teaching regarding the person and work of Jesus Christ.
Protective Anonymity	The practice of avoiding the use of a specific name in order to protect that person. This concept explains why Matthew, Mark, or Luke did not mention certain names but John, writing after their deaths, was free to reveal their identities. This suggests many characters in the gospel story were still living during the time when the Gospels were written.
Proto-orthodox	Ehrman's term for those he believes were one among many groups that had equally legitimate claims to Christianity. According to Ehrman, this group took power and destroyed all the other legitimate forms of Christianity.
Rule of Faith	The early agreed-upon set of core Christian beliefs that demonstrates an early unity in orthodox writings.
Textual criticism	An approach that studies the various manuscripts to evaluate the different copies of ancient documents to determine which reading is closest to the original.
Variants	Differences among the various copies of the biblical manuscripts.

QUICK QUESTION
-AND-
ANSWER GUIDE

Chapter One
Is God Immoral Because He Allows Suffering?

CLAIM 1: It is a contradiction to say that God is sovereign and God is good in view of all the evil in the world.

SHORT RESPONSE: How do you know what "goodness" is in the first place unless we live in a moral universe of which God is the Creator? And is anyone able to sit in judgment over what happens in this world knowing all the reasons why something takes place? Just because suffering doesn't make sense to you or to us doesn't mean there is no God. The freedom people want to choose and rebel against God is what is resisted when consequences come for those acts.

CLAIM 2: The Bible contains many different answers to the problem of why there is suffering in the world, and many of these answers contradict one another.

SHORT RESPONSE: Different instances of suffering may have different explanations. The Bible never says there is one universal reason for all forms of human suffering.

CLAIM 3: The Bible's explanations for suffering and evil are not satisfying.

SHORT RESPONSE: Rational explanations for suffering are not a substitute for faith in a good and loving God. In Jesus, God came to earth and showed that he cares by suffering for us on the cross. "Satisfying" is a value judgment seen differently by different people, not a category that is logically true or false. The fact is no one knows the answers to some of these questions.

CLAIM 4: The God of the Bible is immoral. Therefore, he cannot exist.

SHORT RESPONSE: The problem is not God's immorality; it is our sin and rebellion against the Creator. Rather than deny God's existence, we should repent of our sin and believe in God and the substitute for sin he has provided in the Lord Jesus Christ. How can a God who offers himself on behalf of those who turn their backs on him be immoral?

Chapter Two
Is the Bible Full of Irresolvable Contradictions?

CLAIM 1: The New Testament authors have contradictory points of view on major issues.

SHORT RESPONSE: Diversity does not equal contradiction. The New Testament documents, including the Gospels, reflect different points of view that are mutually complementary rather than contradictory.

CLAIM 2: Attempts to reconcile various events in the New Testament are mistaken because such harmonizations create another account that is different from the ones being read.

SHORT RESPONSE: Harmonization is a legitimate practice used by any good historian to reconstruct the history behind multiple accounts of a series of events. It is an approach used by lawyers in a court of law. Events with depth inevitably have layers and angles to them.

CLAIM 3: The Gospels' chronological differences are historical contradictions.

SHORT RESPONSE: Judged by their own intentions, the Gospels are not guilty as charged because they sometimes choose to present their material topically rather than chronologically. Editorial choices can leave an impression of difference, but they are not demonstrated to be contradictions.

CLAIM 4: The Gospels are so different in detail that they must be deemed in error at numerous points and cannot be viewed as divinely inspired.

SHORT RESPONSE: There are several reasons why the depiction of a given event or teaching may differ in the different Gospels other than indicating error on their part. Only a rigid insistence on literal surface agreement will necessarily conclude that differences in details in the Gospels necessarily involve them in error.

CLAIM 5: The diversity of views within the New Testament indicates that "Jesus was not originally considered to be God in any sense at all . . . he eventually became divine for his followers in some sense before he came to be thought of as equal with God Almighty in an absolute sense."

SHORT RESPONSE: Jesus was not a mere man who became God only later; in Jesus, God took on humanity in the person of Jesus of Nazareth. Within a short decade or two, the early Christians understood that Jesus' identity was intrinsic to the identity of Israel's God and that he was not a second or lesser god but part of God's own being and identity and thus a fitting object of worship. Also, the types of Christology Ehrman claims as contradictory are found side by side, even intertwined, in individual New Testament books such as John's Gospel or Colossians.

The rapid rise of Christianity and the fact that large numbers of Christians were prepared to die for their faith are best accounted by the historical reality of the resurrection of Jesus, not faith in hallucinatory visions of Jesus as risen. This is true especially when one considers that there is no real Jewish precedent to arrive at these conclusions apart from a genuine impetus. The short interval between Jesus' crucifixion and documented worship of Jesus as divine is best explained by Jesus' own claim and actions pointing to deity prior to his violent cross-death and then his resurrection.

Chapter Three
Are the Biblical Manuscripts Corrupt?

CLAIM 1: We don't have the original New Testament manuscripts. We only have copies of copies of copies, so we have no idea if what we now have is what the original manuscripts said.

SHORT RESPONSE: While we don't have the originals, we have an abundance of copies, including a good number of early ones, which enable us to reconstruct the likely original text with a considerable degree of confidence. There is no good reason to believe that significant changes crept in so early in the copying process that they left no trace of the original reading in the copies available to us today.

CLAIM 2: While many variants [differences] in the New Testament manuscripts are insignificant, in many cases the likely original reading is highly disputed, and the most likely rendering affects core theological beliefs.

SHORT RESPONSE: There is substantial agreement on the part of textual critics, whether conservative or otherwise, on what the original manuscripts say in cases such as John's account of the adulterous woman or the longer ending of Mark's Gospel. In the few other cases where there is room for disagreement, no matter which reading is adopted, there is no major doctrinal problem or incongruity in the New Testament documents. None of these textual choices impacts core Christian theology. All that is at stake are how many and which passages make the point.

CLAIM 3: There are more variants in the New Testament manuscripts than there are words in the entire New Testament.

SHORT RESPONSE: The vast majority of New Testament variants are completely inconsequential and involve trivial matters such as spelling errors, easy-to-spot nonsense readings, variation in word order, or Greek article changes. The abundance of manuscripts is a plus, not a minus, because it enables us to reconstruct the original wording with all the more confidence. The textual situation for the New Testament is miles ahead of other classical literature and their textual evidence.

CLAIM 4: Early Christians did not have the means to copy texts accurately.

SHORT RESPONSE: The New Testament documents were copied by scribes, many of whom were sufficiently trained to reproduce originals faithfully and accurately. This existence of a scribal culture is also supported by the widespread practice of abbreviating words denoting deity (the so-called *nomina sacra*) and the Christian preference for the codex (similar to our modern-day books).

CLAIM 5: Orthodox scribes intentionally changed Scripture at such a high doctrinal level that it is impossible to know for certain if an early scribal corruption has occurred in transmission.

SHORT RESPONSE: In the limited number of cases where scribes changed the wording of a particular text to promote a given doctrine (the "orthodox corruption of Scripture") we are able to identify the original wording with a high degree of confidence. However, core doctrine is so distributed across these texts that the overall theological content is not impacted by these contested texts.

CLAIM 6: It is useless to say the Bible is the inspired Word of God when we don't have the original words.

SHORT RESPONSE: We may not have the original New Testament documents, but we almost certainly do have the words the New Testament authors wrote. While God, for reasons of his own, chose not to preserve the original New Testament writings, it seems he did preserve the original wording of these texts in the abundance of manuscripts available to us today. Our object of worship is not the Scriptures; it is Jesus Christ as witnessed to by the Scriptures. The core message shows we can know what God intended.

Chapter Four
Were There Many Christianities?

CLAIM 1: The German scholar Walter Bauer's book *Heresy and Orthodoxy in Earliest Christianity* was "the most important book on the history of early Christianity to appear in the twentieth-century. . . . The argument [made by Bauer] is incisive and authoritative, made by a master of all the surviving early Christian literature."

SHORT RESPONSE: Bauer's book has been widely discredited by historical scholarship. Those who continue to hold to Bauer's view despite the evidence cling to an old, discredited view of the history of early Christianity.

CLAIM 2: Writings from equally early and legitimate "heretical" forms of Christianity do not currently exist because they were destroyed by the proto-orthodox in the first century.

SHORT RESPONSE: This is an argument from silence. There is no evidence (nor can there be) to support this claim one way or another. It is at least as likely that these documents that were supposedly destroyed never existed or were less than prevalent in the first place than that they were destroyed at a later point in time. We do know that in many cases the theology these outside works contend for was removed from the Jewish origins of Jesus and the disciples so as to be unlikely to have roots in the earliest period.

CLAIM 3: Early Christianity was wildly diverse, with no group having a legitimate claim to the "true" form of Christianity.

SHORT RESPONSE: Not true. Early Christianity was widespread and unified in all the core essentials, and any deviation from the true gospel was identified as heretical and as deviating from the commonly received apostolic teaching from the beginning. Of the groups often noted as early and contending, only the Ebionites can be shown to be early. Marcionites and Gnostics arose later.

CLAIM 4: You can never rely on the winners to write an unbiased account of the past. The New Testament is unified because the winning "orthodox" party got to choose what was in its canon.

SHORT RESPONSE: The early Christians didn't have the political or other means to impose their beliefs on others prior to the fourth century. Also, just because someone believes something deeply doesn't mean his or her account is necessarily biased. More than that, the list of books in the New Testament shows evidence of surfacing and being used as significant long before any council named a listing. The New Testament writings showed their importance on their own accord.

CLAIM 5: No standards were in place during the earliest stage of Christianity to distinguish correct from incorrect teachings concerning the person and work of Jesus Christ.

SHORT RESPONSE: This argument can be made only if one disregards our earliest witnesses to belief in Jesus, the Gospels and epistles included in the New Testament. They make crystal clear the fact that from its earliest days the church held to the apostolic teaching concerning the saving death, burial, and resurrection of the Lord Jesus Christ; and no one, not even the apostle Paul or the apostle Peter, was free to tamper with the apostolic message without being branded a heretic. These core points are in place in the thirties when Paul is converted from being a persecutor of the church.

CLAIM 6: Second- and third-century orthodox leaders were innovators rather than guardians of tradition, creating what is now known as orthodoxy.

SHORT RESPONSE: To the contrary, the writings of the church fathers and affirmations such as the rule of faith prove that the ethos of second- and third-century church leaders was to pass on the first-century apostolic teaching rather than to create their own divergent teaching. What these Fathers did do was elaborate, explain, and develop what was in the core.

CLAIM 7: Orthodoxy, which was the product of much later church councils, did not exist in the first century: "For example, none of the apostles claimed that Jesus was 'fully God and fully man,' or that he was 'begotten not made of one substance with the Father,' as the fourth-century Nicene Creed maintained. The victorious group called itself orthodox."

SHORT RESPONSE: If one defines "orthodoxy" as a product of the formulation of fourth-century church councils, then of course orthodoxy is a fourth-century phenomenon. This is circular reasoning. But if "orthodoxy" is defined as the church's commonly agreed-upon teaching concerning the saving significance of the death, burial, and resurrection of Jesus Christ, then this core gospel message was clearly present in the first century, not only in the fourth century. One can see this as early as 1 Corinthians 15:3–5; Romans 1:2–4; 3:19–26; Hebrews 1:1–14; and Ephesians 2:8–10, all works written long before the fourth century.

CLAIM 8: The creation of a canon was one of the strategies used by the proto-orthodox to diminish the authority of other early Christian literature.

SHORT RESPONSE: The concept of a canon is rooted in the Old Testament notion of God's covenant with his people Israel, which issued in old covenant documents recording

the establishment of such a covenant. It follows that Jesus' establishment of a new covenant with his disciples would likewise issue in new covenant documents. The contents of
the canon were not determined arbitrarily but became recognized as special first-century
writings in keeping with apostolic teaching.

Chapter Five
Are Many New Testament Documents Forged?

CLAIM 1: The New Testament Gospels are not historically reliable and are comparable
to the various other "heretical" Gospels because they were not actually written by Jesus'
companions.

SHORT RESPONSE: The canonical Gospels are based on reliable eyewitness testimony carefully monitored by the apostles, Jesus' closest followers during his earthly
ministry. The names of those tied to some books have no compelling reason to have been
chosen unless the tradition knew something about authorship.

CLAIM 2: The first disciples were illiterate and therefore could not have written the
parts of the New Testament attributed to them.

SHORT RESPONSE: This claim insufficiently appreciates several key facts. First,
literacy and education were important to first-century Jews. Second, someone like Peter,
for example, was able to lead a multicultural religious movement, an unlikely feat for "a
backwoods illiterate peasant." Finally, we know that at least some of the New Testament
writers used secretaries.

CLAIM 3: Many of the New Testament books were not really written by the authors to
whom they were ascribed, despite the internal claims of the books themselves. Instead,
they were forged.

SHORT RESPONSE: There is no compelling reason to doubt the traditional attribu-
tion of the New Testament writings to its respective authors, whether Matthew, Mark,
Luke, and John (Gospels), or Paul, Peter, James, Jude, and John (Letters and Revelation).
Forgery was widely frowned upon by Christians in the first century. The statistics of
different vocabulary or theological emphases in particular books attributed to the same
author don't prove forgery. Instead, the range of vocabulary and theological emphases is
more likely due to other factors, such as the occasion and context of the original recip-
ients, the specific topics addressed, the normal variation in vocabulary used by authors
over time, the use of traditional materials and forms in language distinct from the author,
and the possible use of a secretary.

CLAIM 4: Other forms of Christianity are represented in various other writings,
which have equally as valid a claim to Christianity as the twenty-seven canonical New
Testament books.

SHORT RESPONSE: There is a vast difference between the New Testament canonical
writings and apocryphal literature, both in terms of date and content (e.g., the *Gospel
of Thomas* contains a list of sayings but unlike the canonical Gospels has no narrative
framework).

CLAIM 5: The "proto-orthodox" used the canon as a weapon to impose their own brand of theology on all forms of Christianity and eventually succeeded in the fourth century by way of the powerful church of this period.

SHORT RESPONSE: Though achieving a universally recognized 27-book closed New Testament canon was a lengthy process, labeling the canon as a "weapon" used by the church to stamp out legitimate diversity conceals more than it reveals. While the canonicity of some peripheral books remained debated in the third and fourth centuries (as they sometimes still are today), by the end of the first century the core books of the New Testament were widely recognized as canonical. This remarkably early recognition of the core books of the canon—especially surprising in light of no formal or universal structure to declare them so—was due to their production during the apostolic period, their connection with the apostles, and their theology that fit within the story and theology of the Old Testament canon.

INDICES

Name Index

Subject Index

Scripture Index

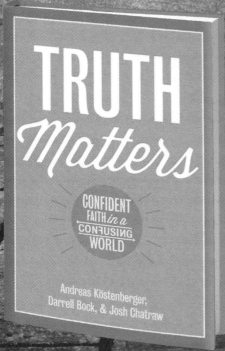